EARLY CHILDHOOD EDUCATION

THE EARLY YEARS CURRICULUM

AND

THE NATIONAL CURRICULUM

Early Years Curriculum Group

Trentham Books

First published in 1989 by Trentham Books Limited

Trentham Books Limited
Westview House
734 London Road
Oakhill
Stoke-on-Trent
Staffordshire
England ST4 5NP

Reprinted 1989
Reprinted 1990 five times
Reprinted 1991
Reprinted 1992 twice
Reprinted 1993
Reprinted 1994
Reprinted 1997

British Cataloguing in Publication Data
A catalogue record for this book is available from the British Library
ISBN: 1 948080 39 6

Cover design by Trentham Print Design Ltd

Printed and typeset in Great Britain by:
Bemrose Shafron (Printers) Limited, Chester

EARLY CHILDHOOD EDUCATION
The Early Years Curriculum and the National Curriculum

This paper has arisen out of the work of the Early Years Curriculum Group whose members are:

Jenny Andreae	- Early Years Inspector, Manchester LEA
Janet Atkin	- University of Nottingham
Tony Bertram	- Worcester College of Higher Education
Sandra Brown	- National Foundation for Educational Research (NFER)
Tina Bruce	- Fellow of Froebel College, Roehampton Institute, London
Sylvia Chard	- formerly College of St. Paul and St. Mary, Cheltenham
Shirley Cleave	- National Foundation for Educational Research (NFER)
Audrey Curtis	- Institute of Education, London, representing OMEP
Wendy Dewhirst	- Leeds Polytechnic
Dorothy Duncan	- Goldsmiths' College, London
Mari Guha	- Goldsmiths' College, London
Peter Heaslip	- Bristol University, representing TACTYC
Vicky Hurst	- Goldsmiths' College, London, representing NCNE
Janet Jones	- British Association for Early Childhood Education (BAECE)
Margaret Lally	- formerly Under Fives Unit, National Children's Bureau
Ann Mason	- Hermitage School, Tower Hamlets
Chris Pascal	- Worcester College of Higher Education
Linda Pound	- Froebel College, Roehampton Institute, London
Gillian Pugh	- Under Fives Unit, National Children's Bureau
Wendy Scott	- Inspector for Early Years, Inner London Education Authority
Pauline Walsh	- Inspector for Early Years, Inner London Education Authority
Marian Whitehead	- Goldsmiths' College, London

This paper has been produced on behalf of the group by:

Tina Bruce	Sylvia Chard	Vicky Hurst
Margaret Lally	Chris Pascal	Wendy Scott

INTRODUCTION

This paper has been written and is endorsed by a group of specialists in education for the early years representing all the major early childhood education organisations, a number of higher education establishments in different parts of the country, and representatives from local education authorities.

The group began meeting in the autumn of 1988 to consider the implications of the national curriculum and assessment at seven for the early years curriculum. It was decided to use the considerable expertise within the group to produce a paper which would:

1. articulate the learning process and context of the curriculum in the early years (based on recent research evidence).

2. state the crucial underlying principles which, when translated into practice, support children's achievement in the early years.

3. demonstrate how current early years practice provides opportunities for experience within the national curriculum framework, illustrated with examples.

4. address issues of progression and continuity in relation to the national curriculum, and show how assessment procedures can be built on existing early years practice.

5. make the links between the principles and practice of early years education and the intentions of the national curriculum.

In the first instance it is intended that the paper should inform the deliberations of the National Curriculum Council, SEAC, and the Department of Education and Science. It is hoped that it will also be given wider circulation so that it is used to support the work of practitioners..

 The Early Years Curriculum Lobby - a group of experts in early childhood education who began meeting in October 1988. They are working together to raise awareness in practitioners, policy makers, and the general public of the importance and special qualities of the curriculum for young children.

The Under Fives Unit at the National Children's Bureau is a national centre for advice, guidance and information on current practice, thinking and research in the under fives field. The unit convened a group representing all the major early childhood education organisations and facilitated the production of this document.

These two groups combined to form the Early Years Curriculum Group which produced this document.

Designed and typeset by: Patrick Short, 79 Spring Road, Letchworth, Herts SG6 3SL

Contents

Cover illustration by children from the nursery class at Brackenbury primary school, London W.6

Contents

FOREWORD

I am delighted to have the opportunity of writing the foreword to this book. Never has there been a greater need, or a more appropriate time for such a publication. Now is the time for informed discussion and for conclusions to be drawn about a curriculum for the early years. It is heartening that a group of specialists from a variety of fields concerned with young children have come together to prepare this book. The examples provided and the clearly drawn nets will be of value to administrators, teachers and parents.

The book expounds the ten key principles underlying the curriculum for the early years. The first principle is that this phase of education is important in its own right. This issue must be linked with the fact that the education of the under fives is not something separate and apart, but is the beginning of the continuum of learning.

Young children learn through play and first hand experience and this book places these two vital elements firmly within the context of the National Curriculum. The thinking behind the curriculum planning describes ways of meeting the needs of young children and of ensuring that attainment targets are met.

The ladder of education can never be secure unless the first rung is firmly in place. We need this book.

Rosemary W. Peacocke
Formerly HMI, Staff Inspector with responsibility for the Early Years

SECTION 1
THE LEARNING PROCESS AND CONTEXT OF THE CURRICULUM IN THE EARLY YEARS

The characteristics of very young children

During their first seven years children grow and develop rapidly and are therefore particularly receptive learners. A six months' age difference between children at this stage is developmentally much more significant than a similar age difference in a group of older children. The younger the children the more important it is that their individual learning needs are identified and planned for, and the less appropriate it is to expect them to conform within a large group.

Very young children have very little life experience to draw on to help them make sense of the world around them, and to enable them to cope with new demands. Early years teachers as well as parents need to offer young children the social and emotional support they need during their first few years at school, to help them to adjust to temporary separation from their family, to the new social context they find themselves in, and to the range of new challenges they encounter within the educational setting. This support is vital if children are to feel confident and secure enough to learn.

However, the needs of very young children are interrelated and it is not possible to separate their need for learning experiences from their need for care and emotional support. As children get older their need for care at school lessens as they become more independent and more able to use past experience to help them make sense of new expectations or challenges.

The learning process

From the time they are born, young children learn through their spontaneous interactions with their environment and with the people around them. The quality of these interactions will inevitably vary, and will determine whether a child feels encouraged to express his or her natural curiosity or discouraged. For example, the child who points excitedly to the first cow she sees and shouts 'look, big doggy' may elicit any number of responses from an adult. She may be ignored, in which case she may eventually learn not to share her discoveries with that adult, or the adult may answer abruptly 'it's not a doggy, it's a cow' and carry on walking, giving the child no time at all to internalise the differences. On the other hand, the adult may stop and encourage the child to look closely and think about the differences between the cow in the field and dogs they have previously seen, and to verbalise those similarities and differences, thereby encouraging the child to continue to express curiosity and interest. This develops the disposition to learn as well as increasing knowledge.

Attitudes and behaviour patterns established during the first seven years of life provide the foundation for future educational and social development. From the example above it is easy to see how children can be motivated or discouraged depending on the response they get to their initial reactions to stimuli. Early years teachers have an important role to play in young children's learning. It is within their power to encourage a feeling of fun and mutual discovery, but it is equally possible for them to create an atmosphere of dull drudgery where children's interests have to wait until adult initiated tasks are completed e.g. 'you can play when you have done your work'. Teachers should value and pursue the ideas and activities which children are drawn towards, in order to be able to create successful learning situations for individuals and small groups of children.

All young children need periods of uninterrupted time in which they can actively explore their environment, set their own challenges, and make their own discoveries. They need opportunities to work collaboratively with their peers, and they need adults who are able to 'tune in to' and extend their natural interests. Above all they need opportunities for learning through play. Through play children practise and consolidate learning, play with ideas, and develop what they know. In their play children also dare to take risks, negotiate, solve problems, initiate, anticipate, rearrange, restate, reflect and integrate and consolidate their knowledge and understanding. When something is fully understood and competence is achieved, they start to play with ideas, and develop humour and wit.

Any adult who has had to learn how to use a new piece of machinery will understand the importance of having some time alone 'playing' with the machine and learning by trial and error and practice. They will also understand that instructions from someone else only become meaningful when a real need for that information is perceived by the learner. For instance, when learning to use a photocopier, the most receptive moment for learning to use the reducing function is when you actually have a document you want to reduce. If someone gives you the information at a time when you do not have this need, it is less likely that the knowledge will be retained. This need for experimentation is much more important for young children, for whom so much knowledge, which adults take for granted, is a mystery. It is also more important that teachers are available to help children to express their discoveries in words, to listen to their questions, and to select the right moment to offer them the support they need to learn more. Later in this document there are examples of how this process is used to teach curriculum subjects in a very positive and meaningful way for individual children.

The learning context

Each child starts school with a unique set of experiences gained at home and in his or her community. A learning environment should respond to each child's need for something familiar, something new and challenging, and something which enables him or her to pursue a current interest. An environment and daily programme which offer maximum choice to individual children in terms of access to equipment and space, use of time, and opportunities for collaboration with others is most appropriate.

A well conceived, well organised resource-based environment, which provides opportunities for discovery across all curriculum areas, is the best means of encouraging personal autonomy and a sense of responsibility. All resources must be maintained carefully and stored in such a way that young children have access at all times and can use them in flexible and imaginative ways; it should be possible for children to have available the equipment they need to be able to pursue their own interests and intentions. The clearing up of materials and areas is a major educational component of their use and daily poses meaningful challenges e.g. why is it that when powder paint is wiped up with a damp cloth it seems to make more mess? How else could it be cleared up? (an excellent opportunity for developing scientific thinking and problem solving).

It is the task of early years teachers to ensure that the learning context they provide offers a broad and stimulating environment which reflects the cultural backgrounds and interests of the children, and provides opportunities for individuals to seek new challenges, as well as to practise and consolidate developing skills and interests. Within an environment of this kind young children and their teachers will be well equipped to accept the challenge of the new initiatives - in fact it is encouraging to note that many of the activities and interactions which children are already experiencing in nursery and infant classes lead to the kind of achievement described in the national curriculum documents.

All of the points discussed in this section are supported by a wealth of theory and recent research evidence. Sources are listed in the bibliography.

THE UNDERLYING PRINCIPLES

The British early childhood curriculum is well established, and has been acknowledged and emulated for many years throughout the world. A catalyst for high quality work with young children and their parents, it is based on important educational principles and founded on good practice. Each generation has translated these principles into practice through an interweaving of theory and current research evidence. This process both supports and develops the early years curriculum.

The early years curriculum is concerned with the child, and the context or setting in which the learning takes place, as well as the content of the learning.

This content should be built on what the children already know. The teacher ensures opportunities for supporting and extending learning and developing knowledge through new experiences. This is most effectively carried out through interaction with the children themselves.

The following principles express the traditions of the curriculum for education in the early years. Although not always expressed in exactly the same terms, they have guided teachers' practice for many years.

Early childhood is valid in itself, and is a part of life, not simply a preparation for work, or for the next stage of education.

The whole child is considered to be important - social, emotional, physical, intellectual and moral development are interrelated.

Learning is holistic and for the young child is not compartmentalised under subject headings.

Intrinsic motivation is valuable because it results in child-initiated learning.

Autonomy and self-discipline are emphasised.

In the early years children learn best through first hand experience.

What children can do, not what they cannot do, is the starting point in children's education.

There is potential in all children which emerges powerfully under favourable conditions.

The adults and children to whom the child relates are of central importance.

The child's education is seen as an interaction between the child and the environment, which includes people as well as materials and knowledge.

These principles carry important implications for practice.

SECTION 3

THE PRACTICAL IMPLICATIONS OF THE NATIONAL CURRICULUM IN THE EARLY YEARS

It is important that the principles of early years education, particularly those which relate to the ways in which young children learn, form the basis for considering how the national curriculum can be implemented. In interpreting the national curriculum we must ensure that these learning processes are acknowledged and strengthened.

The 'webs' which follow provide examples of how the national curriculum can be interpreted in existing good early years practice. All of these 'webs' have as their starting point the needs, interests and experience of children, and assume a learning environment which is well equipped and well organised. The areas of provision and the types of experience illustrated in the webs are ones which should be available to children throughout the 3 - 7 age range. Starting from this base of good early years practice, teachers will be able to interpret the programme of study according to the needs of their children.

It is very important that the webs are seen as examples of planning, and <u>not</u> as prescriptive models. They have been produced to show the range of learning possibilities which are to be found in children's spontaneous interests and play experiences. The involvement of adults needs to be sensitive enough to follow the child's lead and develop ideas within the contexts suggested. It is not effective for adults to impose these experiences on children e.g. by insisting that a child counts the plates in the home corner in a sterile way. Each web includes a paragraph to this effect to ensure that this is fully understood if the web is taken out of the context of the whole document.

There has deliberately been no attempt to standardise the webs, since individual teachers will want to develop their own ways of illustrating how they are relating the national curriculum to the provision they make. Some teachers will want to look at profile components and attainment targets and see how they are covered within existing and planned provision, some will prefer to work through and link the national curriculum to a theme, while others will want to demonstrate progression within particular areas of provision. Many will want to use more than one of these methods, or will devise completely different ones. <u>Whichever approach is chosen, teachers must necessarily take account of children's previous experiences, current interests and developmental needs</u>. In order to do this teachers need in-depth knowledge of child development, and a clear awareness of the learning possibilities within particular activities. Without this knowledge and understanding children's interests are unlikely to be supported and extended.

This variety of approach is reflected in the webs which follow. Four of the webs start from core subject attainment targets, two demonstrate how themes can be used to teach the national curriculum and one shows how an area of provision, the home corner, can offer experience in the core subjects of the national curriculum. Finally there is one which demonstrates how a teacher could assess and extend children's conceptual development within a broad curriculum.

References to attainment targets were correct at the time of going to press.

Home corner, role play, small world

Contents to be designed and explored from first hand experience
teacher and child initiatives

: Bookshop	) lists
: School	) labels
: Newspaper office	) signs
: Post office	) notes
: Bank	) bills
: Station/bank/train	) telegrams
: Cafe	) letters
: Home and imagination	) tickets

Resources - (literacy tours e.g. spaceship, castle)

Tickets, paper (coloured, texture, shapes)

Pens/crayons/pencils/rubber stamps, scissors, glue, paint, cardboard tube etc.

Blocks/Construction

Building and construction of story contexts. Designing, making and explaining models/representations e.g.

: castle

: spaceship

: ladder to touch the moon

: tower

READING level 1

ɛ, both in books and in other

s in familiar contexts

ɪg.

ɔries, or information in

Craft/Creative Art

Story as the impetus for painting, collage, models of story contexts, character and actions (including poems, songs).

Individual and group work: self initiatives, teacher directed

Printing: basic skills: patterns

:   use of variety of artefacts.

Pattern making: brushes/ink wash/paint

ᵈd organisation

ɛls of reading/story

members of the wider

.

ɪd general

ɛ play

resources

:essors

ɪls, adverts

ɔntext

ng, involvement and

ɛating with other adults in

Movement

Drama and role play of stories/poems.

Sequenced narrative by teacher

children

Sequence read by and composed by children, teachers and others. Use of the cards "quietly", "slithery", "sneezed"

Location and positional concepts.

Rᵢythm/sequence sounds/movements.

Songs/jingles/ring games/chants.

ENGLISH IN THE EARLY YEARS

In developing and extending reading, the importance of communication within a genuine and supportive context is crucial. Print related context can be linked to any topic or story theme where careful observation, reading and recording are appropriate to the child's level of understanding. Telling and reading stories/poems to and with young children provides an enjoyable shared experience at school and home.

Through such a medium they come to realise the existence of printed language, learn to understand the function of print and punctuation and develop and extend their potential repertoire of competency in literacy.

The examples given below are not comprehensive, and should not be seen as prescriptive. They are provided to illustrate some of the opportunities for English teaching which exist in the early years classroom.

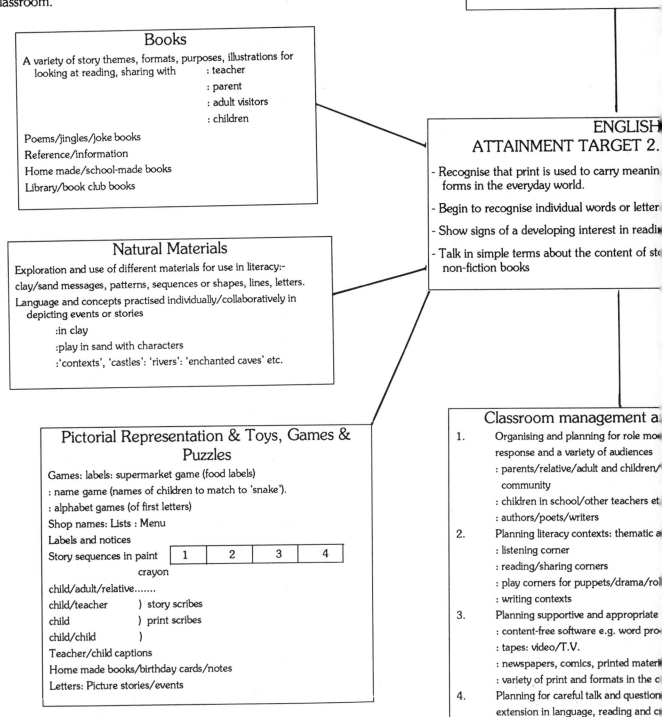

Outdoor

Investigations in the environment:
  : print walks: sky, eye and foot le
  : adverts walk
  : street names/house names
  : letter, word walks: home and so
  : markets: station (bus/train)
  : shops: labels and notices
Playground games: skipping rhymes
  : traditiona
  : letter hop
Outside play: market stalls
  : bus/train station
  : lollipop/zebra cross
  : road safety signs

Books

A variety of story themes, formats, purposes, illustrations for looking at reading, sharing with
  : teacher
  : parent
  : adult visitors
  : children

Poems/jingles/joke books
Reference/information
Home made/school-made books
Library/book club books

Natural Materials

Exploration and use of different materials for use in literacy:-
clay/sand messages, patterns, sequences or shapes, lines, letters.
Language and concepts practised individually/collaboratively in depicting events or stories
  :in clay
  :play in sand with characters
  :'contexts', 'castles': 'rivers': 'enchanted caves' etc.

ENGLISH
ATTAINMENT TARGET 2.

- Recognise that print is used to carry meanin forms in the everyday world.

- Begin to recognise individual words or letter

- Show signs of a developing interest in readi

- Talk in simple terms about the content of sto non-fiction books

Pictorial Representation & Toys, Games & Puzzles

Games: labels: supermarket game (food labels)
: name game (names of children to match to 'snake').
: alphabet games (of first letters)
Shop names: Lists : Menu
Labels and notices
Story sequences in paint

1	2	3	4

  crayon
child/adult/relative.......
child/teacher   ) story scribes
child   ) print scribes
child/child   )
Teacher/child captions
Home made books/birthday cards/notes
Letters: Picture stories/events

Classroom management a

1. Organising and planning for role mo
    response and a variety of audiences
    : parents/relative/adult and children/
      community
    : children in school/other teachers et
    : authors/poets/writers
2. Planning literacy contexts: thematic a
    : listening corner
    : reading/sharing corners
    : play corners for puppets/drama/rol
    : writing contexts
3. Planning supportive and appropriate
    : content-free software e.g. word pro
    : tapes: video/T.V.
    : newspapers, comics, printed materi
    : variety of print and formats in the c
4. Planning for careful talk and question
    extension in language, reading and c
    the context.

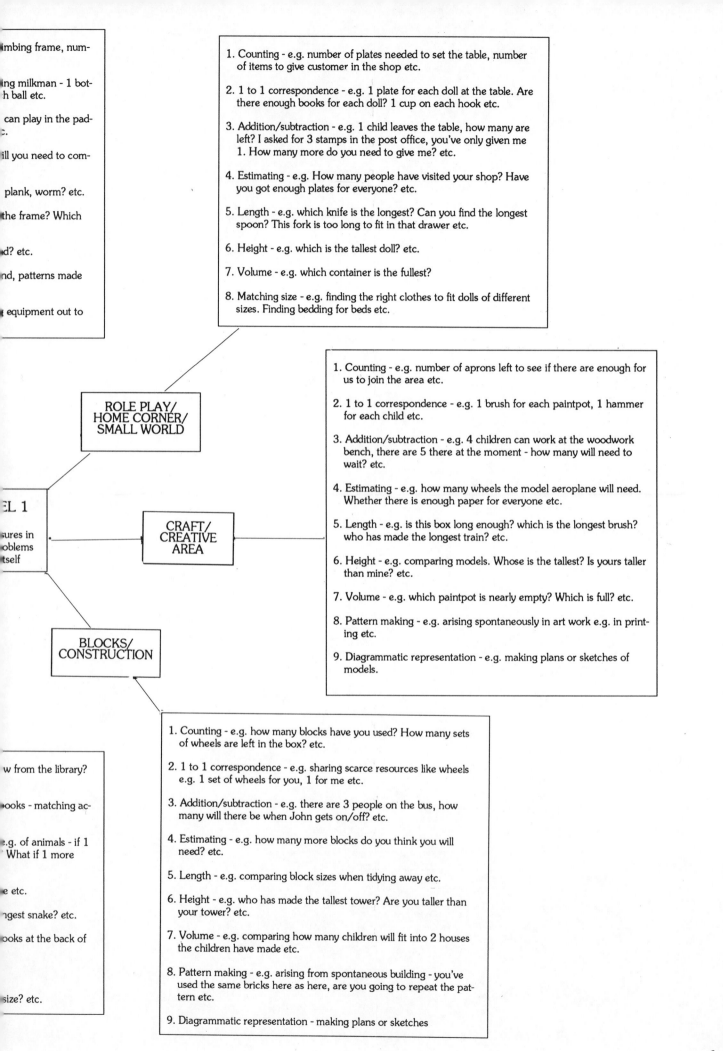

Left partial boxes (cut off):

...mbing frame, num-

...ing milkman - 1 bot-
...h ball etc.

...can play in the pad-
...

...ill you need to com-

...plank, worm? etc.

...the frame? Which

...d? etc.

...nd, patterns made

...equipment out to

...EL 1

...sures in
...oblems
...tself

ROLE PLAY/
HOME CORNER/
SMALL WORLD

CRAFT/
CREATIVE
AREA

BLOCKS/
CONSTRUCTION

Lower left partial box:

...w from the library?

...ooks - matching ac-

...e.g. of animals - if 1
...What if 1 more

...e etc.

...ngest snake? etc.

...ooks at the back of

...size? etc.

ROLE PLAY/HOME CORNER/SMALL WORLD:

1. Counting - e.g. number of plates needed to set the table, number of items to give customer in the shop etc.

2. 1 to 1 correspondence - e.g. 1 plate for each doll at the table. Are there enough books for each doll? 1 cup on each hook etc.

3. Addition/subtraction - e.g. 1 child leaves the table, how many are left? I asked for 3 stamps in the post office, you've only given me 1. How many more do you need to give me? etc.

4. Estimating - e.g. How many people have visited your shop? Have you got enough plates for everyone? etc.

5. Length - e.g. which knife is the longest? Can you find the longest spoon? This fork is too long to fit in that drawer etc.

6. Height - e.g. which is the tallest doll? etc.

7. Volume - e.g. which container is the fullest?

8. Matching size - e.g. finding the right clothes to fit dolls of different sizes. Finding bedding for beds etc.

CRAFT/CREATIVE AREA:

1. Counting - e.g. number of aprons left to see if there are enough for us to join the area etc.

2. 1 to 1 correspondence - e.g. 1 brush for each paintpot, 1 hammer for each child etc.

3. Addition/subtraction - e.g. 4 children can work at the woodwork bench, there are 5 there at the moment - how many will need to wait? etc.

4. Estimating - e.g. how many wheels the model aeroplane will need. Whether there is enough paper for everyone etc.

5. Length - e.g. is this box long enough? which is the longest brush? who has made the longest train? etc.

6. Height - e.g. comparing models. Whose is the tallest? Is yours taller than mine? etc.

7. Volume - e.g. which paintpot is nearly empty? Which is full? etc.

8. Pattern making - e.g. arising spontaneously in art work e.g. in printing etc.

9. Diagrammatic representation - e.g. making plans or sketches of models.

BLOCKS/CONSTRUCTION:

1. Counting - e.g. how many blocks have you used? How many sets of wheels are left in the box? etc.

2. 1 to 1 correspondence - e.g. sharing scarce resources like wheels e.g. 1 set of wheels for you, 1 for me etc.

3. Addition/subtraction - e.g. there are 3 people on the bus, how many will there be when John gets on/off? etc.

4. Estimating - e.g. how many more blocks do you think you will need? etc.

5. Length - e.g. comparing block sizes when tidying away etc.

6. Height - e.g. who has made the tallest tower? Are you taller than your tower? etc.

7. Volume - e.g. comparing how many children will fit into 2 houses the children have made etc.

8. Pattern making - e.g. arising from spontaneous building - you've used the same bricks here as here, are you going to repeat the pattern etc.

9. Diagrammatic representation - making plans or sketches

MATHS IN THE EARLY YEARS

This is an example of how a programme of study for Maths attainment target 1, level 1 is covered within provision in the early years classroom. Situations arise spontaneously in children's play and can be developed through the sensitive involvement of adults. Adult expertise lies in being able to select the appropriate moment for intervention and to build on the immediate interests of the child. It is not suggested that the examples here are either comprehensive or prescriptive; they are offered purely as examples of the types of situations/interventions which provide opportunities for Maths teaching. This model could be applied to all profile components in each subject area.

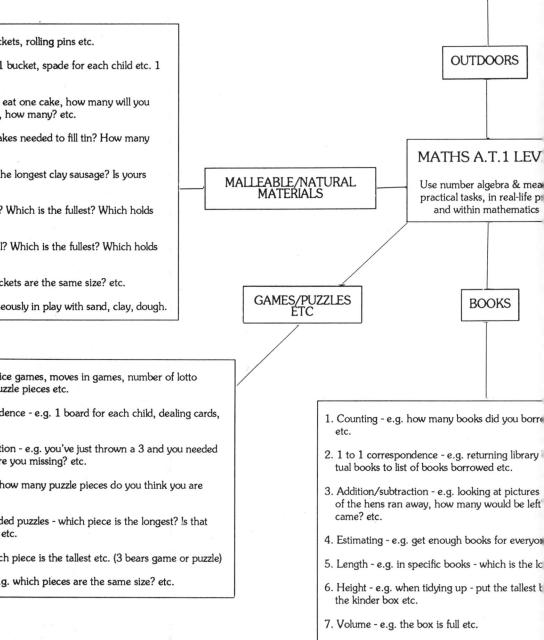

(OUTDOORS)

1. Counting - e.g. number of children on a c... ber of bats, balls and cycles etc.

2. 1 to 1 correspondence - e.g. playing at be... tle of milk for each customer. 1 bat for ea...

3. Addition/subtraction - e.g. only 6 childre... dling pool, how many will have to wait? e...

4. Estimating - e.g. how many more crates v... plete the wall? etc.

5. Length - e.g. which is the longest shadow...

6. Height - e.g. which child is the highest on... flower is the tallest? etc.

7. Volume - e.g. which bucket is fullest of sa...

8. Pattern making - e.g. wet feet on the grou... by shoe soles etc.

9. Diagrammatic representation - e.g. puttin... match adult drawn plan.

MALLEABLE/NATURAL MATERIALS

1. Counting - e.g. number of buckets, rolling pins etc.

2. 1 to 1 correspondence - e.g. 1 bucket, spade for each child etc. 1 dough cake for each tin etc.

3. Addition/subtraction - e.g. if I eat one cake, how many will you have left? If you make 1 more, how many? etc.

4. Estimating - e.g. how many cakes needed to fill tin? How many children in sand? etc.

5. Length - e.g. Who has made the longest clay sausage? Is yours longer than mine? etc.

6. Height - e.g. Is the bucket full? Which is the fullest? Which holds the most? etc.

7. Volume - e.g. Is the bucket full? Which is the fullest? Which holds the most? etc.

8. Matching size - e.g. Which buckets are the same size? etc.

9. Patterns - e.g. arising spontaneously in play with sand, clay, dough.

MATHS A.T.1 LEV...

Use number algebra & mea... practical tasks, in real-life p... and within mathematics

GAMES/PUZZLES ETC

BOOKS

1. Counting - e.g. dice games, moves in games, number of lotto pieces needed, puzzle pieces etc.

2. 1 to 1 correspondence - e.g. 1 board for each child, dealing cards, one for you etc.

3. Addition/subtraction - e.g. you've just thrown a 3 and you needed a 4, how many are you missing? etc.

4. Estimating - e.g. how many puzzle pieces do you think you are missing? etc.

5. Length - e.g. graded puzzles - which piece is the longest? Is that longer than that? etc.

6. Height - e.g. which piece is the tallest etc. (3 bears game or puzzle)

7. Matching size - e.g. which pieces are the same size? etc.

1. Counting - e.g. how many books did you borr... etc.

2. 1 to 1 correspondence - e.g. returning library... tual books to list of books borrowed etc.

3. Addition/subtraction - e.g. looking at pictures... of the hens ran away, how many would be left... came? etc.

4. Estimating - e.g. get enough books for everyo...

5. Length - e.g. in specific books - which is the lo...

6. Height - e.g. when tidying up - put the tallest... the kinder box etc.

7. Volume - e.g. the box is full etc.

8. Matching size - e.g. which books are the same...

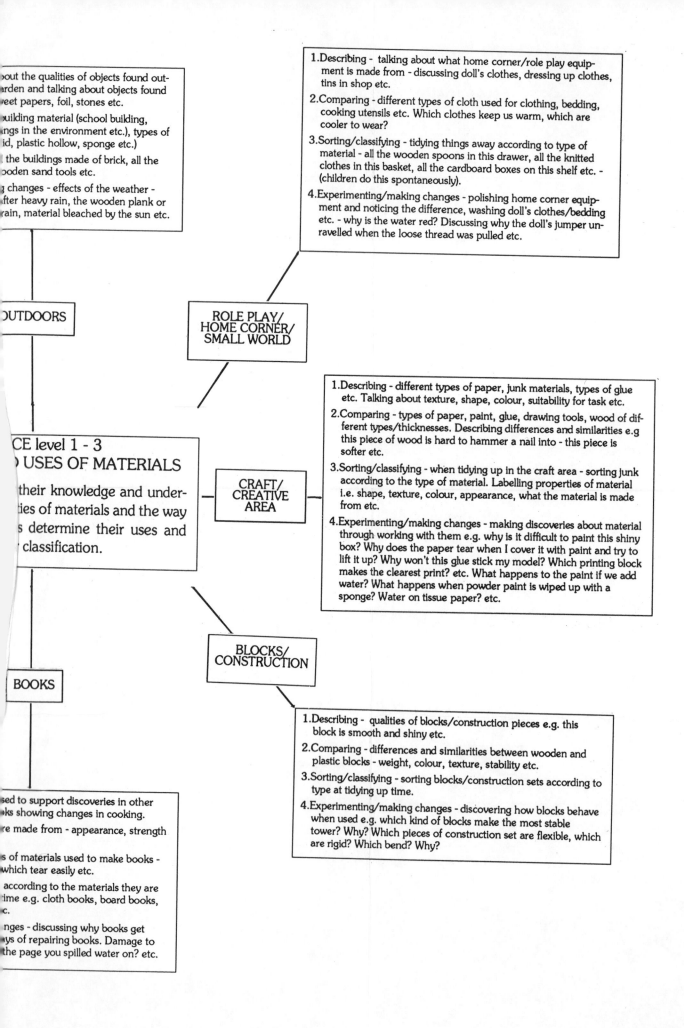

Top right box (connected to ROLE PLAY/HOME CORNER/SMALL WORLD):

1. Describing - talking about what home corner/role play equipment is made from - discussing doll's clothes, dressing up clothes, tins in shop etc.
2. Comparing - different types of cloth used for clothing, bedding, cooking utensils etc. Which clothes keep us warm, which are cooler to wear?
3. Sorting/classifying - tidying things away according to type of material - all the wooden spoons in this drawer, all the knitted clothes in this basket, all the cardboard boxes on this shelf etc. - (children do this spontaneously).
4. Experimenting/making changes - polishing home corner equipment and noticing the difference, washing doll's clothes/bedding etc. - why is the water red? Discussing why the doll's jumper unravelled when the loose thread was pulled etc.

Left box (OUTDOORS):

...bout the qualities of objects found out-
...rden and talking about objects found
...eet papers, foil, stones etc.

...building material (school building,
...ngs in the environment etc.), types of
...id, plastic hollow, sponge etc.)

...the buildings made of brick, all the
...ooden sand tools etc.

...g changes - effects of the weather -
...fter heavy rain, the wooden plank or
...rain, material bleached by the sun etc.

Node: OUTDOORS

Node: ROLE PLAY/ HOME CORNER/ SMALL WORLD

Centre-left box:

...CE level 1 - 3
... USES OF MATERIALS

...their knowledge and under-
...ies of materials and the way
...s determine their uses and
...classification.

Node: CRAFT/ CREATIVE AREA

Craft/Creative Area box:

1. Describing - different types of paper, junk materials, types of glue etc. Talking about texture, shape, colour, suitability for task etc.
2. Comparing - types of paper, paint, glue, drawing tools, wood of different types/thicknesses. Describing differences and similarities e.g this piece of wood is hard to hammer a nail into - this piece is softer etc.
3. Sorting/classifying - when tidying up in the craft area - sorting junk according to the type of material. Labelling properties of material i.e. shape, texture, colour, appearance, what the material is made from etc.
4. Experimenting/making changes - making discoveries about material through working with them e.g. why is it difficult to paint this shiny box? Why does the paper tear when I cover it with paint and try to lift it up? Why won't this glue stick my model? Which printing block makes the clearest print? etc. What happens to the paint if we add water? What happens when powder paint is wiped up with a sponge? Water on tissue paper? etc.

Node: BLOCKS/ CONSTRUCTION

Node: BOOKS

Books box:

...sed to support discoveries in other
...ks showing changes in cooking.

...re made from - appearance, strength

...s of materials used to make books -
...which tear easily etc.

...according to the materials they are
...ime e.g. cloth books, board books,
...c.

...nges - discussing why books get
...ys of repairing books. Damage to
...the page you spilled water on? etc.

Blocks/Construction box:

1. Describing - qualities of blocks/construction pieces e.g. this block is smooth and shiny etc.
2. Comparing - differences and similarities between wooden and plastic blocks - weight, colour, texture, stability etc.
3. Sorting/classifying - sorting blocks/construction sets according to type at tidying up time.
4. Experimenting/making changes - discovering how blocks behave when used e.g. which kind of blocks make the most stable tower? Why? Which pieces of construction set are flexible, which are rigid? Which bend? Why?

SCIENCE IN THE EARLY YEARS

This is an example of how a programme of study including Science attainment target 6 (types and uses of materials) can be covered within the provision in an early years classroom. There are many spontaneous opportunities for science teaching in a resource-based setting as children experiment with materials and make their own discoveries. Skilled teachers use these rich opportunities to extend children's understanding, and to plan additional work, linked to programmes of study, which build on interests brought by the children. The examples given are neither comprehensive nor prescriptive, but suggest just a few relevant opportunities for learning that may arise.

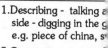

1. Describing - talking a
   side - digging in the g
   e.g. piece of china, s
2. Comparing - types of
   climbing frames, buil
   ball (rubber hollow/s
3. Sorting/classifying - a
   sponge balls, all the v
4. Experimenting/makin
   what happens to soli
   the nail left out in the

---

1. Describing - talking about the qualities of sand, water, dough, clay etc. Discussing taste, smell, appearance, texture of cooking ingredients etc.
2. Comparing - wet and dry sand, clay and dough, dough made with plain flour and dough made with self-raising flour, cooked and uncooked pasta etc.
3. Sorting/classifying - tidying away sand/water/clay tools - all the wooden ones here, all the metal ones here etc.
4. Experimenting/making changes - what happens when you squash dough; you try to make a castle with wet and dry sand; you put clay through a garlic press; you add water to clay; you heat chocolate; you put water in the freezer or bread dough in a warm place? etc. Experiments to find out:- what floats and sinks; which fabrics let most water through; which substances dissolve etc.

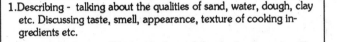

MALLEABLE/NATURAL MATERIALS

SCIE
A.T.6 TYPES A

Pupils should devel
standing of the pro
properties of mate
form the basis for t

GAMES/PUZZLES ETC

1. Describing - properties of materials games and puzzles are made from.
2. Comparing - this puzzle is stronger than this one; this board bends and this one doesn't etc.
3. Sorting/classifying - when tidying up games and puzzles - all the wooden puzzles in this pile etc.
4. Experimenting/making changes - making new pieces of a game to replace lost or broken ones. Experimenting to find the most suitable materials. Discussing what has happened to a cardboard lotto piece which has been chewed or sucked!

Story and reference books
areas of provision e.g. bo
1. Describing - what books
   etc.
2. Comparing - different typ
   which ones are strongest
3. Sorting/classifying - book
   made from - at tidying up
   paper backs, hard backs
4. Experimenting/making cl
   broken, and discovering v
   books - what happened te

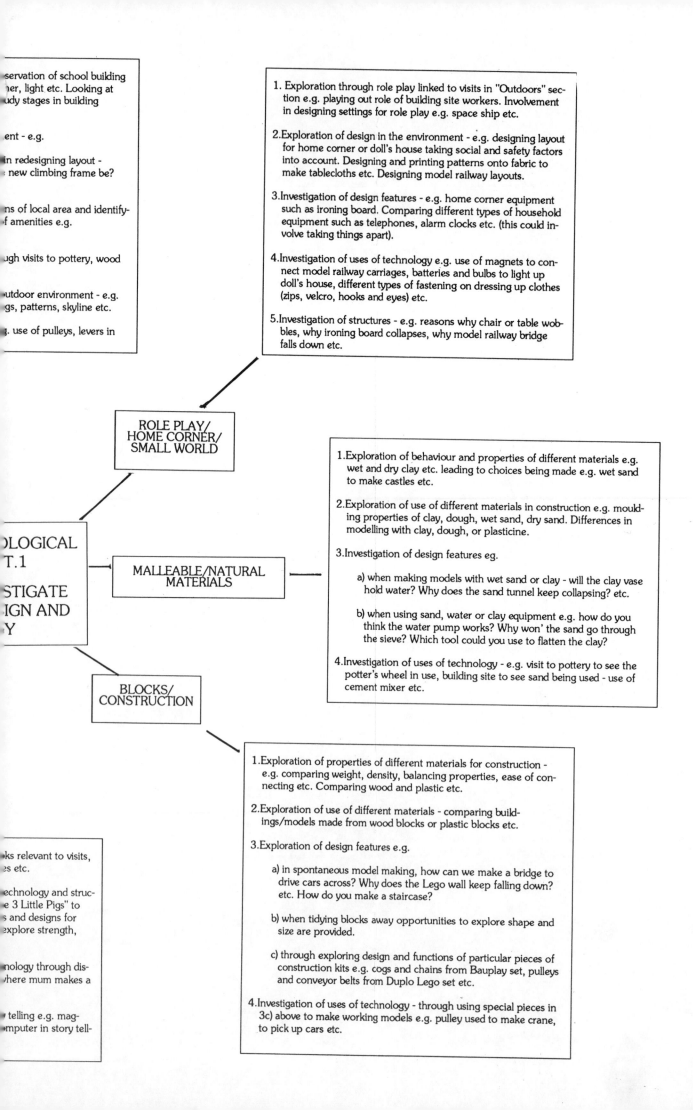

...servation of school building
...her, light etc. Looking at
...udy stages in building

...ent - e.g.

...in redesigning layout -
... new climbing frame be?

...ns of local area and identify-
...f amenities e.g.

...ugh visits to pottery, wood

...utdoor environment - e.g.
...gs, patterns, skyline etc.

...g. use of pulleys, levers in

1. Exploration through role play linked to visits in "Outdoors" section e.g. playing out role of building site workers. Involvement in designing settings for role play e.g. space ship etc.

2. Exploration of design in the environment - e.g. designing layout for home corner or doll's house taking social and safety factors into account. Designing and printing patterns onto fabric to make tablecloths etc. Designing model railway layouts.

3. Investigation of design features - e.g. home corner equipment such as ironing board. Comparing different types of household equipment such as telephones, alarm clocks etc. (this could involve taking things apart).

4. Investigation of uses of technology e.g. use of magnets to connect model railway carriages, batteries and bulbs to light up doll's house, different types of fastening on dressing up clothes (zips, velcro, hooks and eyes) etc.

5. Investigation of structures - e.g. reasons why chair or table wobbles, why ironing board collapses, why model railway bridge falls down etc.

ROLE PLAY/
HOME CORNER/
SMALL WORLD

...OLOGICAL
...T.1

...STIGATE
...IGN AND
...Y

MALLEABLE/NATURAL
MATERIALS

1. Exploration of behaviour and properties of different materials e.g. wet and dry clay etc. leading to choices being made e.g. wet sand to make castles etc.

2. Exploration of use of different materials in construction e.g. moulding properties of clay, dough, wet sand, dry sand. Differences in modelling with clay, dough, or plasticine.

3. Investigation of design features eg.

   a) when making models with wet sand or clay - will the clay vase hold water? Why does the sand tunnel keep collapsing? etc.

   b) when using sand, water or clay equipment e.g. how do you think the water pump works? Why won' the sand go through the sieve? Which tool could you use to flatten the clay?

4. Investigation of uses of technology - e.g. visit to pottery to see the potter's wheel in use, building site to see sand being used - use of cement mixer etc.

BLOCKS/
CONSTRUCTION

...ks relevant to visits,
...es etc.

...echnology and struc-
... 3 Little Pigs" to
...s and designs for
...explore strength,

...nology through dis-
...here mum makes a

... telling e.g. mag-
...mputer in story tell-

1. Exploration of properties of different materials for construction - e.g. comparing weight, density, balancing properties, ease of connecting etc. Comparing wood and plastic etc.

2. Exploration of use of different materials - comparing buildings/models made from wood blocks or plastic blocks etc.

3. Exploration of design features e.g.

   a) in spontaneous model making, how can we make a bridge to drive cars across? Why does the Lego wall keep falling down? etc. How do you make a staircase?

   b) when tidying blocks away opportunities to explore shape and size are provided.

   c) through exploring design and functions of particular pieces of construction kits e.g. cogs and chains from Bauplay set, pulleys and conveyor belts from Duplo Lego set etc.

4. Investigation of uses of technology - through using special pieces in 3c) above to make working models e.g. pulley used to make crane, to pick up cars etc.

DESIGN AND TECHNOLOGY IN THE EARLY YEARS

Below is an example of how Design and Technology ATI can be covered within provision in the early years classroom. Many situations arise spontaneously during children's activity, which can be extended to develop their understanding of aspects of design and technology - e.g. the wheeled toy which loses a wheel. There are also many opportunities for involving children in adult led projects which arise out of the need to solve a particular problem e.g. the new pet needing a run. The examples given below should not be seen as either comprehensive or prescriptive - they are offered purely to show the range of situations which can provide the adult with opportunities for design and technology teaching. The skills of the teacher lie in seizing these opportunities when they arise.

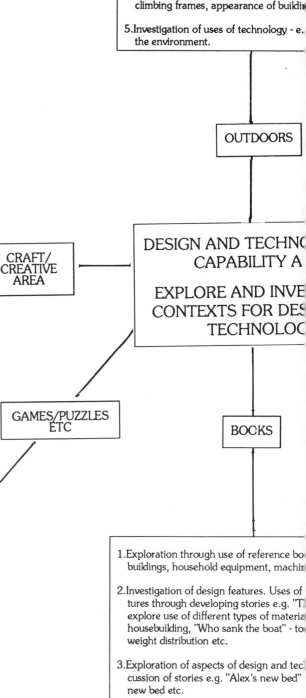

1. Exploration of building design - e.g. o▮ with reference to safety, storage, wea▮ school plan. Visits to building site to s▮ process etc.

2. Exploration of designs in the environm▮

   a) outdoor play areas - involvement where would the best place for th▮ etc.

   b) immediate locality - looking at pl▮ ing amenities - reasons for siting ▮ playground, car park etc.

3. Exploration of design in industry - thro▮ yard, craft workshop, printers etc.

4. Investigation of design features in the ▮ climbing frames, appearance of buildi▮

5. Investigation of uses of technology - e.▮ the environment.

OUTDOORS

---

1. Exploration of properties of materials - e.g. comparing absorbency, card will bend, wood will not. Some paint runs, other paint does not.

2. Exploration of use of materials - e.g. which is the best paper for painting? Which glue is the strongest? Selecting from a wide range of junk materials the most appropriate material for a model, collage etc.

3. Exploration of use and effects of tools - e.g. paint brushes of different thicknesses, scissors, staples, hole punchers, hammers, saws, vices, screwdrivers, sandpaper etc. etc.

4. Exploration of design features - e.g. :-

   a) in spontaneous representative creative work - the child needs to observe (or have observed) closely the object s/he is trying to represent in paint, junk materials, wood etc.

   b) through exploring and seeing the potential of particular pieces of junk material in designing models etc. - e.g. "this box has a see-through lid. I could use it to make a window" etc.

   c) repairing broken equipment.

5. Investigation of uses of technology - observing use of more sophisticated tools e.g. on visits to workshops to see use of: drills, electrical equipment, such as sanders, sewing machines etc.

6. Learning about the need for plans - through making something (e.g.rabbit run) from adult drawn plans.

CRAFT/ CREATIVE AREA

DESIGN AND TECHN▮ CAPABILITY A▮

EXPLORE AND INVE▮ CONTEXTS FOR DE▮ TECHNOLO▮

GAMES/PUZZLES ETC

BOOKS

---

1. Exploration of design features and process - e.g. by making simple puzzles from card. Visiting craft workshops to see wooden puzzles being made etc.

2. Exploration of use of different materials - e.g comparing card and wood puzzles for durability; comparing different quality wood puzzles for strength; comparing puzzles where picture is directly painted onto wood with those where puzzles are painted on paper which is then stuck onto wood. etc.

3. Investigation of uses of technology in games - e.g. matching games which make use of batteries, bells and/or buzzers to indicate correct match, sound lotto games using tape recorder, use of computer games etc. Talking about pictures on puzzles which illustrate uses of technology in the environment.

---

1. Exploration through use of reference bo▮ buildings, household equipment, machir▮

2. Investigation of design features. Uses of tures through developing stories e.g. "T▮ explore use of different types of materia▮ housebuilding, "Who sank the boat" - to▮ weight distribution etc.

3. Exploration of aspects of design and tec▮ cussion of stories e.g. "Alex's new bed" new bed etc.

4. Exploration of uses of technology in stor▮ netic story props, taped stories, use of ▮ ing etc.

The study of a topic or theme

'Projects', 'topics' or 'themes'? - a note about terminology

All three of these terms, 'projects', 'topics' and 'themes', are widely used in reference to interdisciplinary learning in the early years. Sometimes teachers favour the use of one particular term rather than the others. Such variation seems to arise from two main sources: geographical location and age of children referred to. For example, in Oxfordshire the term 'project work' is frequently used; in Gloucestershire, 'topic work'; and in London, 'thematic work'. In referring to the work of the youngest children, the word 'theme' is more likely to be used, for the infants 'topic' and for the older primary children, the term 'project'. However, all three terms are used by writers on the subject in reference to the work of children throughout the primary age range. Books on interdisciplinary work in the curriculum most frequently use the word 'topic' and least frequently use the word 'theme'. In recent D.E.S. publications ('Curriculum Matters', and 'From Policy into Practice', for instance) 'topic' is the most frequently used term. In this introduction to interdisciplinary learning we have used all three terms.

We have tried to use the terms appropriately from a semantic and syntactical point of view: for example, you might plan and undertake a project, develop a theme and study or explore a topic. In our use of the terms we have also particularly tried to convey the curriculum practice we are intending to support.

In the early years, children learn particularly successfully through their interest in real events, objects or people. They learn about a topic or theme such as 'growing plants' or 'building a house' through active exploration and first hand experience. Sometimes the whole class is involved in such learning, for instance through a visit to a farm or a supermarket. Sometimes only groups or individual children make a close study: for example, how a bicycle works or how to build and set up a bird table. Not all children have to undertake the same activities in such class or group projects and there is much genuine exchange of information in class discussion, on wall displays, in social play and in drawing and writing collected in 'class books'.

Project work is particularly valued by some teachers because it enables children actively to develop interests over a period of time. It builds on the experience and knowledge the children have acquired outside school, for example, knowledge of shopping, travelling or personal hygiene routines for keeping healthy. The sustained interest shown by children in thematic activities enables them to study in some depth and to develop their knowledge and ideas in a variety of ways.

Through their study of a topic or theme the teacher helps children to try out for themselves what they know and can do, in pursuit of their own questions and real purposes. Class or group projects provide the context to help children make genuine use of their academic skills, for example, writing a letter to arrange an interview with a nurse, or a police officer. They also offer opportunities for children to work at different levels of challenge. Children can practise some skills independently with proficiency. On other occasions they can try solving problems which make heavy demands on them. The study of everyday objects, places, or events is enriched by role play opportunities which enable the children to explore and 'try out' new information they encounter. Themes suggest props which can elaborate the play activity and the language used. The project approach thus increases the potential of social play in the classroom to develop children's knowledge and understanding.

The teacher's planning for the study of a topic begins with knowledge of the children. An opened-ended web diagram may then be constructed to show an outline of key experiences through which their knowledge and understanding can be developed. The teacher also plans with the children's current levels of skill in mind so that they can work independently, accept the challenges of problem solving and develop confidence. The children should also be actively involved in planning and implementing projects.

In the process of project work, many of the attainment targets of the national curriculum can be addressed in ways which are most likely to ensure effective leaning. It is important for children to learn from direct experience in a variety of ways in the classroom. Access to the curriculum for young children depends on the teacher adapting the learning environment of the classroom to ensure as far as possible that the full range of particular learning needs are met. With this in mind the interdisciplinary study of themes or topics through class project work offers important opportunities for implementing the programmes of study recommended in the national curriculum proposals in all areas of the curriculum.

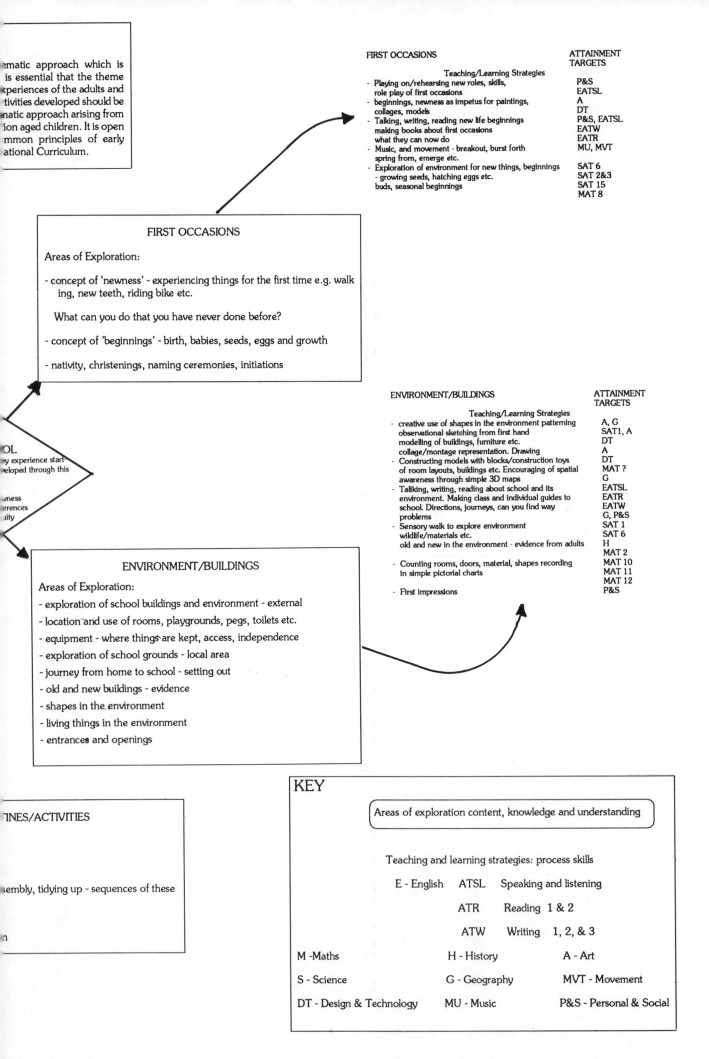

ematic approach which is
is essential that the theme
xperiences of the adults and
tivities developed should be
natic approach arising from
ion aged children. It is open
mmon principles of early
ational Curriculum.

FIRST OCCASIONS

Areas of Exploration:

- concept of 'newness' - experiencing things for the first time e.g. walking, new teeth, riding bike etc.

  What can you do that you have never done before?

- concept of 'beginnings' - birth, babies, seeds, eggs and growth

- nativity, christenings, naming ceremonies, initiations

FIRST OCCASIONS   **ATTAINMENT TARGETS**

Teaching/Learning Strategies

Teaching/Learning Strategies	Attainment Targets
- Playing on/rehearsing new roles, skills, role play of first occasions	P&S EATSL
- beginnings, newness as impetus for paintings, collages, models	A DT
- Talking, writing, reading new life beginnings making books about first occasions what they can now do	P&S, EATSL EATW EATR
- Music, and movement - breakout, burst forth spring from, emerge etc.	MU, MVT
- Exploration of environment for new things, beginnings - growing seeds, hatching eggs etc. buds, seasonal beginnings	SAT 6 SAT 2&3 SAT 15 MAT 8

OL

y experience start·
eloped through this

·ness
·erences
·ity

ENVIRONMENT/BUILDINGS

Areas of Exploration:
- exploration of school buildings and environment - external
- location and use of rooms, playgrounds, pegs, toilets etc.
- equipment - where things are kept, access, independence
- exploration of school grounds - local area
- journey from home to school - setting out
- old and new buildings - evidence
- shapes in the environment
- living things in the environment
- entrances and openings

ENVIRONMENT/BUILDINGS   **ATTAINMENT TARGETS**

Teaching/Learning Strategies

Teaching/Learning Strategies	Attainment Targets
- creative use of shapes in the environment patterning observational sketching from first hand modelling of buildings, furniture etc. collage/montage representation. Drawing	A, G SAT1, A DT A
- Constructing models with blocks/construction toys of room layouts, buildings etc. Encouraging of spatial awareness through simple 3D maps	DT MAT ? G
- Talking, writing, reading about school and its environment. Making class and individual guides to school. Directions, journeys, can you find way problems	EATSL EATR EATW G, P&S
- Sensory walk to explore environment wildlife/materials etc. old and new in the environment - evidence from adults	SAT 1 SAT 6 H MAT 2
- Counting rooms, doors, material, shapes recording in simple pictorial charts	MAT 10 MAT 11 MAT 12
- First impressions	P&S

INES/ACTIVITIES

sembly, tidying up - sequences of these

n

KEY

Areas of exploration content, knowledge and understanding

Teaching and learning strategies: process skills

E - English   ATSL   Speaking and listening

            ATR   Reading 1 & 2

            ATW   Writing   1, 2, & 3

M -Maths   H - History   A - Art

S - Science   G - Geography   MVT - Movement

DT - Design & Technology   MU - Music   P&S - Personal & Social

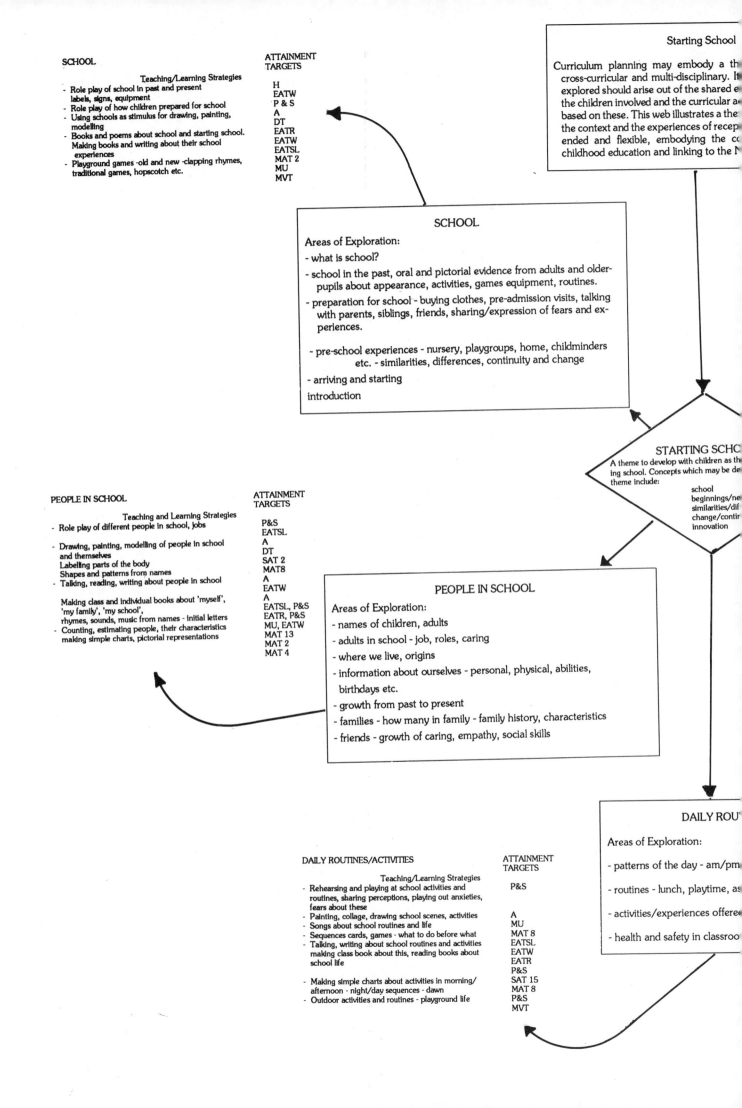

SCHOOL

Teaching/Learning Strategies
- Role play of school in past and present
  labels, signs, equipment
- Role play of how children prepared for school
- Using schools as stimulus for drawing, painting,
  modelling
- Books and poems about school and starting school.
  Making books and writing about their school
  experiences
- Playground games -old and new -clapping rhymes,
  traditional games, hopscotch etc.

ATTAINMENT
TARGETS

H
EATW
P & S
A
DT
EATR
EATW
EATSL
MAT 2
MU
MVT

SCHOOL

Areas of Exploration:

- what is school?

- school in the past, oral and pictorial evidence from adults and older-
  pupils about appearance, activities, games equipment, routines.

- preparation for school - buying clothes, pre-admission visits, talking
  with parents, siblings, friends, sharing/expression of fears and experiences.

- pre-school experiences - nursery, playgroups, home, childminders
  etc. - similarities, differences, continuity and change

- arriving and starting

introduction

Starting School

Curriculum planning may embody a th
cross-curricular and multi-disciplinary. I
explored should arise out of the shared e
the children involved and the curricular a
based on these. This web illustrates a the
the context and the experiences of recep
ended and flexible, embodying the c
childhood education and linking to the

STARTING SCHC

A theme to develop with children as th
ing school. Concepts which may be de
theme include:

school
beginnings/ne
similarities/dif
change/contir
innovation

PEOPLE IN SCHOOL

Teaching and Learning Strategies
- Role play of different people in school, jobs

- Drawing, painting, modelling of people in school
  and themselves
  Labelling parts of the body
  Shapes and patterns from names
- Talking, reading, writing about people in school

  Making class and individual books about 'myself',
  'my family', 'my school',
  rhymes, sounds, music from names - initial letters
- Counting, estimating people, their characteristics
  making simple charts, pictorial representations

ATTAINMENT
TARGETS

P&S
EATSL
A
DT
SAT 2
MAT8
A
EATW
A
EATSL, P&S
EATR, P&S
MU, EATW
MAT 13
MAT 2
MAT 4

PEOPLE IN SCHOOL

Areas of Exploration:

- names of children, adults

- adults in school - job, roles, caring

- where we live, origins

- information about ourselves - personal, physical, abilities,

  birthdays etc.

- growth from past to present

- families - how many in family - family history, characteristics

- friends - growth of caring, empathy, social skills

DAILY ROUTINES/ACTIVITIES

Teaching/Learning Strategies
- Rehearsing and playing at school activities and
  routines, sharing perceptions, playing out anxieties,
  fears about these
- Painting, collage, drawing school scenes, activities
- Songs about school routines and life
- Sequences cards, games - what to do before what
- Talking, writing about school routines and activities
  making class book about this, reading books about
  school life

- Making simple charts about activities in morning/
  afternoon - night/day sequences - dawn
- Outdoor activities and routines - playground life

ATTAINMENT
TARGETS

P&S

A
MU
MAT 8
EATSL
EATW
EATR
P&S
SAT 15
MAT 8
P&S
MVT

DAILY ROU

Areas of Exploration:

- patterns of the day - am/pm

- routines - lunch, playtime, as

- activities/experiences offere

- health and safety in classroo

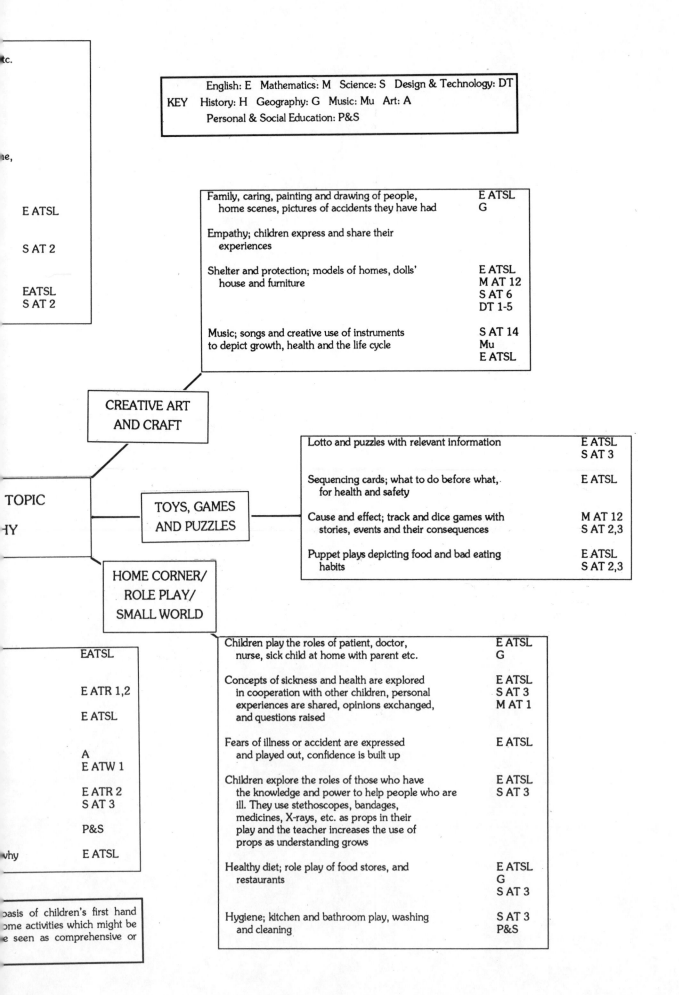

etc.

le,

E ATSL

S AT 2

EATSL
S AT 2

KEY

English: E   Mathematics: M   Science: S   Design & Technology: DT
History: H   Geography: G   Music: Mu   Art: A
Personal & Social Education: P&S

Family, caring, painting and drawing of people, home scenes, pictures of accidents they have had	E ATSL G
Empathy; children express and share their experiences	
Shelter and protection; models of homes, dolls' house and furniture	E ATSL M AT 12 S AT 6 DT 1-5
Music; songs and creative use of instruments to depict growth, health and the life cycle	S AT 14 Mu E ATSL

CREATIVE ART
AND CRAFT

Lotto and puzzles with relevant information	E ATSL S AT 3
Sequencing cards; what to do before what, for health and safety	E ATSL
Cause and effect; track and dice games with stories, events and their consequences	M AT 12 S AT 2,3
Puppet plays depicting food and bad eating habits	E ATSL S AT 2,3

TOPIC

HY

TOYS, GAMES
AND PUZZLES

HOME CORNER/
ROLE PLAY/
SMALL WORLD

EATSL

E ATR 1,2

E ATSL

A
E ATW 1

E ATR 2
S AT 3

P&S

why   E ATSL

oasis of children's first hand
ome activities which might be
e seen as comprehensive or

Children play the roles of patient, doctor, nurse, sick child at home with parent etc.	E ATSL G
Concepts of sickness and health are explored in cooperation with other children, personal experiences are shared, opinions exchanged, and questions raised	E ATSL S AT 3 M AT 1
Fears of illness or accident are expressed and played out, confidence is built up	E ATSL
Children explore the roles of those who have the knowledge and power to help people who are ill. They use stethoscopes, bandages, medicines, X-rays, etc. as props in their play and the teacher increases the use of props as understanding grows	E ATSL S AT 3
Healthy diet; role play of food stores, and restaurants	E ATSL G S AT 3
Hygiene; kitchen and bathroom play, washing and cleaning	S AT 3 P&S

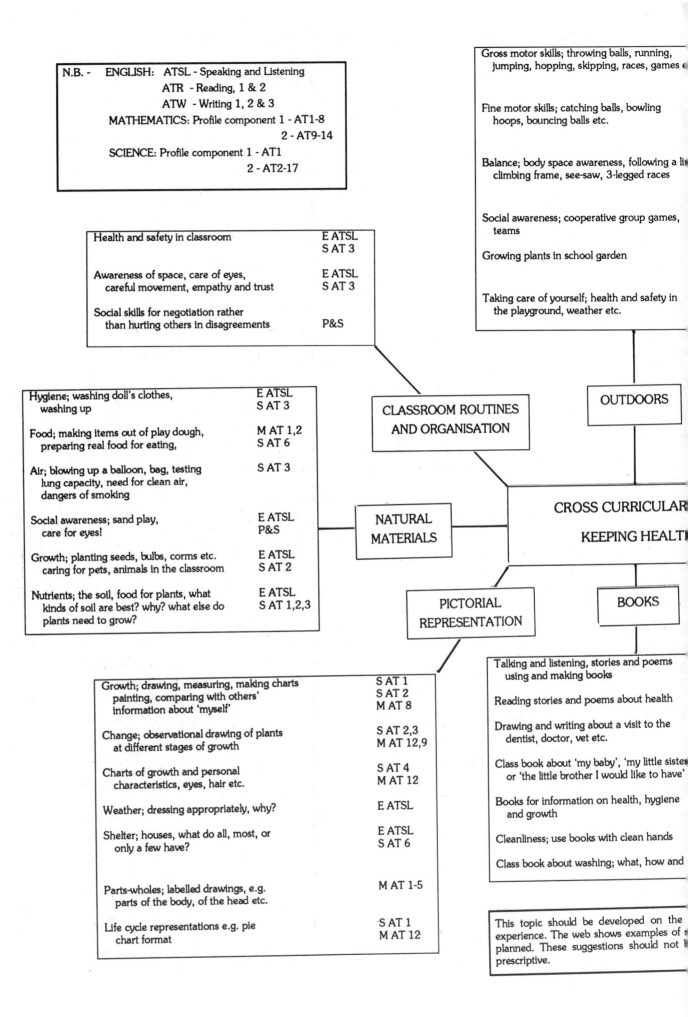

N.B. - ENGLISH: ATSL - Speaking and Listening
           ATR - Reading, 1 & 2
           ATW - Writing 1, 2 & 3
      MATHEMATICS: Profile component 1 - AT1-8
                                    2 - AT9-14
      SCIENCE: Profile component 1 - AT1
                               2 - AT2-17

Health and safety in classroom	E ATSL S AT 3
Awareness of space, care of eyes, careful movement, empathy and trust	E ATSL S AT 3
Social skills for negotiation rather than hurting others in disagreements	P&S

Hygiene; washing doll's clothes, washing up	E ATSL S AT 3
Food; making items out of play dough, preparing real food for eating,	M AT 1,2 S AT 6
Air; blowing up a balloon, bag, testing lung capacity, need for clean air, dangers of smoking	S AT 3
Social awareness; sand play, care for eyes!	E ATSL P&S
Growth; planting seeds, bulbs, corms etc. caring for pets, animals in the classroom	E ATSL S AT 2
Nutrients; the soil, food for plants, what kinds of soil are best? why? what else do plants need to grow?	E ATSL S AT 1,2,3

Gross motor skills; throwing balls, running, jumping, hopping, skipping, races, games e

Fine motor skills; catching balls, bowling hoops, bouncing balls etc.

Balance; body space awareness, following a li climbing frame, see-saw, 3-legged races

Social awareness; cooperative group games, teams

Growing plants in school garden

Taking care of yourself; health and safety in the playground, weather etc.

CLASSROOM ROUTINES AND ORGANISATION

OUTDOORS

NATURAL MATERIALS

CROSS CURRICULAR

KEEPING HEALTH

PICTORIAL REPRESENTATION

BOOKS

Growth; drawing, measuring, making charts painting, comparing with others' information about 'myself'	S AT 1 S AT 2 M AT 8
Change; observational drawing of plants at different stages of growth	S AT 2,3 M AT 12,9
Charts of growth and personal characteristics, eyes, hair etc.	S AT 4 M AT 12
Weather; dressing appropriately, why?	E ATSL
Shelter; houses, what do all, most, or only a few have?	E ATSL S AT 6
Parts-wholes; labelled drawings, e.g. parts of the body, of the head etc.	M AT 1-5
Life cycle representations e.g. pie chart format	S AT 1 M AT 12

Talking and listening, stories and poems using and making books

Reading stories and poems about health

Drawing and writing about a visit to the dentist, doctor, vet etc.

Class book about 'my baby', 'my little siste or 'the little brother I would like to have'

Books for information on health, hygiene and growth

Cleanliness; use books with clean hands

Class book about washing; what, how and

This topic should be developed on the experience. The web shows examples of planned. These suggestions should not prescriptive.

asures

ength - e.g. get the longest scarf from the dressing up. Is your
irt longer than hers? etc.

eight - e.g. which doll is the tallest? etc.

olume - e.g. which bowl is the fullest? etc.

atching size e.g. - clothes to doll, bedding to bed etc.

ebra

terns - discussing patterns on curtains, tablecloths etc. Print-
g patterns on cloths etc.

ndling data

idying pretend food into tins according to types selected by
d e.g. all fruit, all cakes etc. Tidying dolls' clothes. Children
this spontaneously.

robabilities - e.g. what might happen if we leave the tin there?
c.

DESIGN AND TECHNOLOGY

Contexts for design and technology

Many contexts arise spontaneously in the home corner for adults to develop
with children e.g. the need for a new washing machine, tablecloth, vase,
bedcover; the need to repair a piece of equipment e.g. ironing board,
cupboard doors etc.

Formulating proposals and choosing design

Children and adults often work together to discuss how they would make or
repair a piece of equipment e.g. How was the ironing board joined together
before? What pattern shall we have on the cloth? Which colour? etc.

Developing the design and planning

Children and adults could work together to select appropriate materials (e.g.
will a washing machine made from a box be durable?), make a plan if
appropriate; and think about who could do what when e.g. in one nursery
the children thought the home corner needed a front door with a letter box.
Adults and children worked together at all stages over a number of weeks to
plan, measure, shop for wood, and construct a frame with a doorway. This
one project incorporated experience in all core curriculum subjects.

Making artefacts etc.

Children and adults work together to make the required equipment e.g. printing
on white material for a table cloth; making a vase from clay etc.

Appraising processes, outcomes and effects

Once complete, children can be encouraged to reflect on the success or
otherwise of the venture e.g. how does the tablecloth improve the appearance
of the home corner? Does the clay vase hold water? Why has the door fallen
off the cardboard washing machine already? etc.

f materials - talking about what con-
from etc. Cooking in the home
e change.

here - effect of the weather on the light
r. Are the radiators on or not? Shadows

that slide down the draining board?
ing board collapse? etc. How will we
ard?

agnetism - provide magnetic fridge at-
erimentation. Where can you fix these?
eas with batteries and bulbs. Fixing a

10. Scientific aspects of information technology, including
microelectronics - use of old radio, T.V. and telephone.
Use of working distance telephones. Taking radios etc.
apart.

11. Energy transfers - polishing using heated and cold wax.
Bread making. What clothes will the doll need if you take
her outside? Use of the toy thermometer etc.

12. Sound and music - spontaneous sound making e.g.
stirring, banging things together. Use of working radio etc.

13. Using light and electromagnetic radiation - exploring
reflections - in mirror, in shiny things, windows, spoons
(both sides). Exploring shadows. Rainbow effects etc.

14. The Earth in space - why is the light on today? Changes
in plant growth etc.

Experience of the core curriculum subjects offered by the home corner

The well organised, richly resourced home corner can offer a wealth of opportunity for experience of the core subjects of the national curriculum. The diagram below gives some examples of how children's experiences in the home corner can demonstrate their achievement of the level 1 attainment targets.

It is not suggested that these examples should be seen as being either comprehensive or prescriptive. They are offered purely to demonstrate some of the situations which provide adults with the opportunity to observe children's developing understanding and competence. Skilled adults ensure that appropriate, well resourced provision is available, involve themselves sensitively in children's activity, and build on and extend children's interests and understanding.

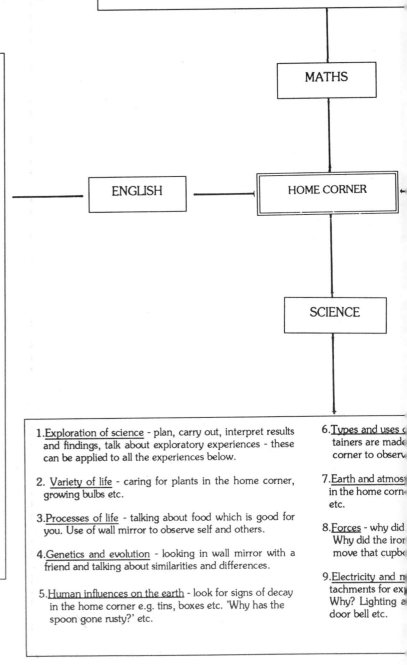

Number

1. Counting - e.g. number of plates needed, number of dolls at table etc.

2. 1 to 1 correspondence - e.g. has everyone got a knife, fork and plate? Are there enough beds for each doll? etc.

3. Addition and subtraction - e.g. you've got 3 knives, how many more do you need? How many are left? etc.

4. Estimating - e.g. how many dolls have we got? etc.

Shape and space

1. Organising home corner equipment - how will it fit in? Which piece of furniture will fit in here? etc.

2. Matching plates, cutlery etc. from different sets etc.

3. Choosing the cloth to fit the table (e.g. round, square or rectangular cloth to fit square table?).

4. Organising different shape containers/boxes in cupboards etc.

5. Language of space - e.g. it's on top of the cupboard, under the table, behind the ironing board, next to the sink etc.

MATHS

ENGLISH — **HOME CORNER**

SCIENCE

Speaking and Listening

1. Working co-operatively with another child - explaining, asking, instructing, reporting, negotiating, sharing ideas.

2. Responding to instructions given to others e.g. you get the forks etc.

3. Working through disputes and reaching a compromise.

4. Joining in talk to develop imaginative play, acting out stories etc.

Writing

1. Writing 'shopping lists', letters and other notices, demonstrating ability to write.

2. Beginning to notice letters and words in the environment and use these in the above.

Reading

1. Recognising that print in the home corner (e.g. on tins, posters etc.) means something e.g. 'this says baked beans' etc.

2. Using phone directory, calendar in a meaningful way - e.g. 'I'm finding my nan's number' etc.

3. Interest in being read to e.g. 'What does this say?' etc.

4. Reading bedtime stories to dolls, teddies etc.

5. Recognising some words/letters e.g. 'This says cornflakes', 'this is my name' etc.

6. Using information books e.g. recipe books etc.

---

1. Exploration of science - plan, carry out, interpret results and findings, talk about exploratory experiences - these can be applied to all the experiences below.

2. Variety of life - caring for plants in the home corner, growing bulbs etc.

3. Processes of life - talking about food which is good for you. Use of wall mirror to observe self and others.

4. Genetics and evolution - looking in wall mirror with a friend and talking about similarities and differences.

5. Human influences on the earth - look for signs of decay in the home corner e.g. tins, boxes etc. 'Why has the spoon gone rusty?' etc.

6. Types and uses ... tainers are made ... corner to observ...

7. Earth and atmos... in the home corn... etc.

8. Forces - why did ... Why did the iron ... move that cupb...

9. Electricity and m... tachments for ex... Why? Lighting a... door bell etc.

The awareness of many teachers of the characteristic ways of thinking of children aged between three and six or seven, leads them to plan to support and extend the experiences which children choose for themselves. These experiences are frequently attempts to come to terms with complex and abstract ideas which children approach in different ways.

This process involves children in experimenting broadly across the curriculum where they can seek for themselves appropriate opportunities to generalise and refine their growing understanding, and requires the teacher to trust, enable and support children as they make choices and direct their own learning. Teachers have an important responsibility to raise their own awareness of the needs of individual children through sensitive observation, and to use these observations to evaluate on a regular basis the provision they are making to ensure that it is responsive to these needs.

The example given demonstrates how, over a period of time, children's ideas about being inside and outside can be explored and developed in physical, social, emotional and moral as well as intellectual terms. Although difficult to account for and explain, this reflection on boundaries and belonging is a fundamental kind of exploration of the world, and a central part of cognitive and emotional growth.

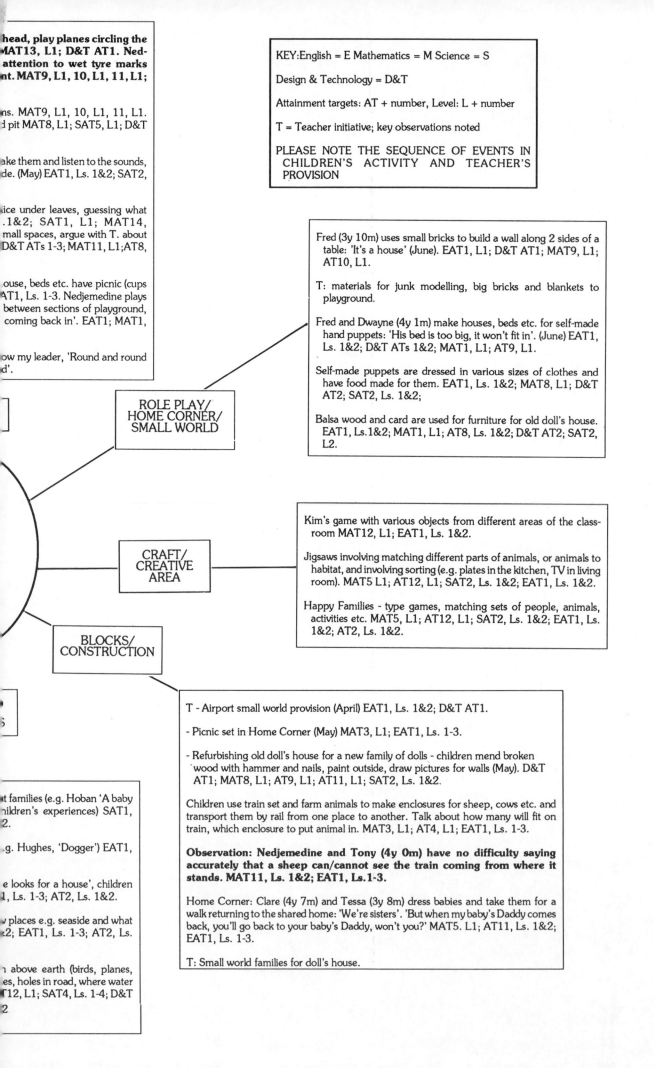

head, play planes circling the MAT13, L1; D&T AT1. Ned- attention to wet tyre marks nt. MAT9, L1, 10, L1, 11, L1;

ns. MAT9, L1, 10, L1, 11, L1. d pit MAT8, L1; SAT5, L1; D&T

ake them and listen to the sounds, de. (May) EAT1, Ls. 1&2; SAT2,

ice under leaves, guessing what .1&2; SAT1, L1; MAT14, mall spaces, argue with T. about D&T ATs 1-3; MAT11, L1;AT8,

ouse, beds etc. have picnic (cups AT1, Ls. 1-3. Nedjemedine plays between sections of playground, coming back in'. EAT1; MAT1,

ow my leader, 'Round and round d'.

KEY:English = E Mathematics = M Science = S

Design & Technology = D&T

Attainment targets: AT + number, Level: L + number

T = Teacher initiative; key observations noted

PLEASE NOTE THE SEQUENCE OF EVENTS IN CHILDREN'S ACTIVITY AND TEACHER'S PROVISION

ROLE PLAY/ HOME CORNER/ SMALL WORLD

Fred (3y 10m) uses small bricks to build a wall along 2 sides of a table: 'It's a house' (June). EAT1, L1; D&T AT1; MAT9, L1; AT10, L1.

T: materials for junk modelling, big bricks and blankets to playground.

Fred and Dwayne (4y 1m) make houses, beds etc. for self-made hand puppets: 'His bed is too big, it won't fit in'. (June) EAT1, Ls. 1&2; D&T ATs 1&2; MAT1, L1; AT9, L1.

Self-made puppets are dressed in various sizes of clothes and have food made for them. EAT1, Ls. 1&2; MAT8, L1; D&T AT2; SAT2, Ls. 1&2;

Balsa wood and card are used for furniture for old doll's house. EAT1, Ls.1&2; MAT1, L1; AT8, Ls. 1&2; D&T AT2; SAT2, L2.

CRAFT/ CREATIVE AREA

Kim's game with various objects from different areas of the class-room MAT12, L1; EAT1, Ls. 1&2.

Jigsaws involving matching different parts of animals, or animals to habitat, and involving sorting (e.g. plates in the kitchen, TV in living room). MAT5 L1; AT12, L1; SAT2, Ls. 1&2; EAT1, Ls. 1&2.

Happy Families - type games, matching sets of people, animals, activities etc. MAT5, L1; AT12, L1; SAT2, Ls. 1&2; EAT1, Ls. 1&2; AT2, Ls. 1&2.

BLOCKS/ CONSTRUCTION

---

t families (e.g. Hoban 'A baby hildren's experiences) SAT1, 2.

.g. Hughes, 'Dogger') EAT1,

e looks for a house', children I, Ls. 1-3; AT2, Ls. 1&2.

places e.g. seaside and what .2; EAT1, Ls. 1-3; AT2, Ls.

n above earth (birds, planes, es, holes in road, where water 12, L1; SAT4, Ls. 1-4; D&T 2

T - Airport small world provision (April) EAT1, Ls. 1&2; D&T AT1.

- Picnic set in Home Corner (May) MAT3, L1; EAT1, Ls. 1-3.

- Refurbishing old doll's house for a new family of dolls - children mend broken wood with hammer and nails, paint outside, draw pictures for walls (May). D&T AT1; MAT8, L1; AT9, L1; AT11, L1; SAT2, Ls. 1&2.

Children use train set and farm animals to make enclosures for sheep, cows etc. and transport them by rail from one place to another. Talk about how many will fit on train, which enclosure to put animal in. MAT3, L1; AT4, L1; EAT1, Ls. 1-3.

Observation: Nedjemedine and Tony (4y 0m) have no difficulty saying accurately that a sheep can/cannot see the train coming from where it stands. MAT11, Ls. 1&2; EAT1, Ls.1-3.

Home Corner: Clare (4y 7m) and Tessa (3y 8m) dress babies and take them for a walk returning to the shared home: 'We're sisters'. 'But when my baby's Daddy comes back, you'll go back to your baby's Daddy, won't you?' MAT5. L1; AT11, Ls. 1&2; EAT1, Ls. 1-3.

T: Small world families for doll's house.

ENCOURAGING CHILDREN'S
CONCEPTUAL DEVELOPMENT
WITHIN EARLY YEARS
PROVISION

This work arises from classroom observation of children's developing ideas about the world, in which objects and events are conceptually linked through associations of movement, shape and spatial relationship. The children's active engagement with varied expression and representation of their ideas is the starting point which can be sensitively developed by the teacher.

Observation: Assunta (3y 4m) has trouble settling in. T: explains how to find play and representational materials and encourages her and her mother to explore provision; T: involves other children in focus on classification and ordering of materials, with games about what goes where and children's self-made labels (big/medium/small brushes, for instance). Children encouraged to think about how to maintain resources. EAT1, Ls.1&2; SAT5, Ls.1&2; AT2, Ls.1&2; Mat1,L1; AT8,L1; AT12, Ls.1&2; D&T AT1.

T - planes in sand, boats in water. (April). Children circle planes above heads, fill boats with stones (April)

Maireaid fills containers repeatedly with sand and water, packing them to the limits. MAT8, L1; SAT5, L1; D&T, AT1 (May)

T - sits at clay, talking of guessing what's inside e.g. an egg: children make shapes of eggs, presents etc. and conceal them in clay, asking others to guess. (June) EAT1, Ls.1&2; D&T AT1; MAT!$, Ls.1&2; SAT5, Ls.1&2.

Children make clay very wet and use for finger painting: Assunta produces ovals by natural movement of arms, adds facial features - 'It's Giorgio (brother)'. EAT1, L1; SAT3, L1; MAT13, L1; D&T AT1.

Maireaid (4y 3m) paints rough oval, repeatedly circling with the brush (April) 'It's an airplane'. EAT1, L1; D&T AT1; MAT13, L1; AT9, L1.

Maireaid paints many more ovals; after absence on holiday places dots inside to represent named members of her family (May). MAT13, L1; MAT9, L1; D&T AT!; EAT1, L1.

T - additional painting materials. Maireaid continues ovals in range of media until end of term.

Nedjemedine draws a circle with dots inside, says 'round and round the nursery!' EAT1, L1; MAT13, L1; AT9, L1; D&T AT1. (June)

Observation: Maireaid, Nedjemedine and Fred draw frequent ovals but choose rectangular paper even when circular and oval pieces are available - the act of imposing the pattern, not accepting another's prior patterning, seems to be an essential ingredient. MAT12 L1; D&T AT1.

CLASSROOM ROUTINES
AND ORGANISATION

NATURAL
MATERIALS

PICTORIAL
REPRESENTATION

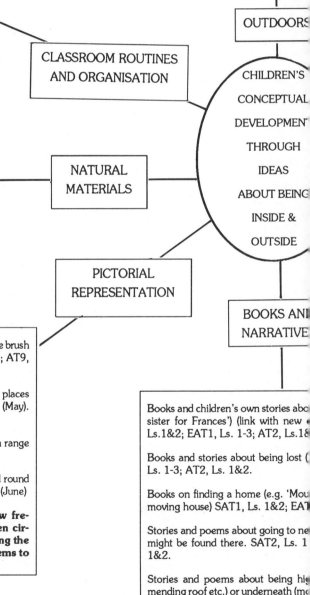

CHILDREN'S

CONCEPTUAL

DEVELOPMENT

THROUGH

IDEAS

ABOUT BEING

INSIDE &

OUTSIDE

OUTDOORS

BOOKS AND
NARRATIVE

Observation: children see planes ove playground (April) EAT1, Ls. 1&2; jemedine (4y 6m) on bicycle draws enclosing particular items of equipm MAT13, L1.

(April) T: chalk provided. N. encircles ite Maireaid fills and overfills containers in sa AT1. (May)

T - packets of seeds for sowing. Children s guessing whether big or small seeds are ins L1; MAT14, Ls. 1&2.

Children dig for worms, search for woo might be hidden (June). EAT1, L Ls.1&2.Children play games of hiding in whether she could fit in too. EAT1, Ls.1-3 Ls. 1&2; At9, L1.

Fred, Linda and Sally use planks to make for 4 people) MAT3, L1; D&T ATs 1-3; E game of bicycling in and out of small gate calling over low fence 'I'm outside' or 'I'm L1. (June)

T: ring games, hiding/guessing games, fo the playground', 'There were ten in the b

Books and children's own stories abo sister for Frances') (link with new Ls.1&2; EAT1, Ls. 1-3; AT2, Ls.1&

Books and stories about being lost (Ls. 1-3; AT2, Ls. 1&2.

Books on finding a home (e.g. 'Mou moving house) SAT1, Ls. 1&2; EAT

Stories and poems about going to ne might be found there. SAT2, Ls. 1 1&2.

Stories and poems about being hig mending roof etc.) or underneath (mc goes from bathroom). MAT11, L1; A AT1-2; EAT1, Ls. 1-3; AT2, Ls. 1&

PROGRESSION, OBSERVATION AND ASSESSMENT

Progression from the child's point of view

Young children learn most effectively when they are actively involved in first hand experience. Their learning is energised by curiosity and interest. When children are involved and interested they are acting and thinking with the competence and knowledge which they already possess. This developmental principle has far-reaching implications for the curriculum. It means that activities designed to promote learning should be concerned primarily with knowledge content which builds on experiences which are familiar to the children. There is evidence that children's play and conversation is more elaborate when they are thinking about familiar 'real world' situations rather than unfamiliar or abstract ones.

Progression and variety of experience

In order to develop a full understanding of a concept a child must have relevant learning experiences in different situations. In order to develop a skill there must be an opportunity to practise it and apply it in many contexts. Children, as indeed all learners, have to generalise from experience in order to apply knowledge appropriately in new situations. It is particularly helpful for young children to have many opportunities to become familiar with the range of potential applications of new competence. The teacher therefore needs to provide a variety of relevant experiences for children in the classroom to develop knowledge and skills. This variety enables children to play, explore, elaborate knowledge, practise and apply skills in the solution of a range of problems they seek out for themselves.

TWO EXAMPLES FROM THE CLASSROOM

Example 1: Planting seeds with a group

In a group of children who are planting seeds, there will be some for whom it may be the first time. Others may have had the opportunity to do it before or to see parents growing seedlings for the garden at home. For all the children it may be the first time they have looked closely at different kinds of seeds. They can feel grass seeds, cress, sunflower, candytuft and broad bean seeds. They can observe and notice similarities and differences. As they do this the teacher talks with individuals according to their past experience and consequent level of attainment of knowledge. For one child the talk is about the range and number of sizes and shapes among the seeds (Science: AT1 L1; AT2 L1; AT6 L1; Maths: AT1 L1; AT2 L2; AT8 L1). The teacher encourages the use of words such as smooth, pointed, dark coloured, markings etc. With another child the teacher asks about how different these seeds were from the ones planted last time and encourages comparison of items present with ones recalled (Science: ATs at L1 as above, and AT1 L2). As this child talks about his garden at home he displays considerable knowledge of how plants grow in gardens and what conditions they need (Science: AT2 L2; AT2 L3). With still another child the parts of the seed may be more interesting, for example the skin of the broad bean (presoaked for speed of germination), the sections inside (cotyledons), the embryonic root bud seen with a magnifying glass (conversation includes reference to genetics, Science: AT4 L5; also AT3 L3, L4 & L5).

As the seeds grow, the responses of the children will vary from astonished delight at the first appearance of green grass shoots coming up out of the earth in a yoghurt pot (Science: AT2 L1), to a discussion of geotropism and phototropism as the broadbean root, in spite of being turned around, insists on growing downwards and the shoot upwards (Science: AT2 L3, or L6?). The discussion with the teacher does not vary in communicative quality in each case, in the sense that the teacher and the child will be equally committed to the verbal exchange. The difference will lie in the nature and amount of factual information in relation to the levels of interest and understanding of the child involved, whether the teacher is building on understanding which is at attainment level one, two or three.

Example 2: A longitudinal case study of progression in one child

It may be helpful to take another possible example to illustrate progression. Most children at age 7 are likely to be assessed at Level 2 in respect of most of the attainment targets. Let us consider a child who is at Level 1 in November 1990 in Science Attainment Target 2. The child, Ruth, has not long been in school and is aged five years and six months old. She lives in a high rise flat in a densely populated urban area of a major city. Taking a look into the classroom over some time we can see how progression typically takes place in the case of one child. Reference is made to another child, Darren, who provides a realistic contrast.

November 14th: The teacher has brought some vegetables into school for the children to work with as part of a project on shopping. A group of children are looking closely at brussels sprouts, carrots, potatoes and a red cabbage. They notice the different colours and shapes and Ruth comments on the similarity between the cabbage and a sprout with reference to leaves and stem and the different patterns to be seen in the two cross sections which have been cut. (Science: AT1 L1; AT2 L1)

Another child, Darren, comments that the sprout's leaves are getting limp because it has been picked off its roots. He thinks it grows like the cabbage, down on the earth. The teacher gets the book with pictures of cabbages and brussels sprouts growing in a garden. Ruth, who has very little experience of plant growth, seems at first very interested , but quickly loses interest and returns to printing round patterns with the carrot sections. Darren, however, who has more experience of gardens enters into a long conversation with the teacher and two other children with gardens at home about what his grandfather grows and how he has to water the garden when the weather is dry. (Ruth - Science: AT1 & AT2 L1; Darren - Science AT1 & AT2 L2)

The conversation continues (reflecting the different attainment levels: Darren with the experience and understanding for Level 2 attainment, Ruth for Level1): "Carrots grow down in the earth and so do potatoes" the teacher says. "I know, I helped my grandad dig some up the other day" said Darren. "Me and my mum bought some potatoes at the shop yesterday" said Ruth, "ooh, look at this colour!" as she printed with an onion section. The teacher extends Ruth's remark, "Yes, the onion makes lovely curved stripey patterns, doesn't it?"

December14th: At the end of the Autumn term, one month later, the children plant bulbs to leave in school over the Christmas holidays. Darren comments on the daffodil bulb being like an onion. The teacher brings an onion into school again so that they can examine it inside. She explains how the layers get used up by the plant as the shoot and the flower grow in the spring.

January 15th: The children look after the now sprouting bulbs by keeping the soil moist. Ruth is very interested in the growth of the shoots and is stroking the strong green shoot with her fingers. Darren comes up and says "my grandad says you mustn't touch plants like that!" "Why not?" says Ruth, stopping. "Because your hands are too hot and the shoots can easily get broken and they'll die." "Mine's the biggest! I'm going to give it more water." "You'd better not give it too much though" suggests the teacher, overhearing the conversation, "too much water can make the bulb rot."

<u>February 12th</u>: "Teacher, come and look, my daffodil plant's breaking!" They go and look, "Don't worry about that, it's only one leaf that has grown too tall and needs some support to stand up. Find a stick in that box, about four hand spans long and we'll tie the leaves to it." Once the plant is safely supported Ruth is reassured. "What's this bit?" "That's the flower bud." "I thought it would be yellow." "The bud is green at first. Look, this is just a thin skin covering the petals. It protects them as the bud grows. When the flower is ready to open, the skin will split and the petals will grow yellow and spread out." (Science: AT2 L1/L2)

<u>February 24th</u>: The children are sitting on the carpet discussing the progress of the crocus, daffodils and hyacinths on the shelf nearby. The class have become very interested in the bulbs as there seems to be something new to notice every day as the different kinds of flowerheads develop. At several group times each week some reference, either brief, or more extended, is made to the plants. On this occasion Ruth is telling the rest of the class about the sequence of events leading to the opening of the first daffodil flower bud.

<u>March 15th</u>: On arrival in the morning, before registration, Ruth comments to the teacher, "Me and my mum, we saw some daffodils in a garden just up the street today." "Is my daffodil going to have any more flowers?" she asks, looking at the limp remains of her plant in the pot on the windowsill. The teacher explains "the bulbs come out much earlier if you grow them indoors like we did here. If they grow in the garden, they come up and flower later because it is so much colder." "I liked growing my own daffodil" said Ruth, wistfully, "Can we grow some more bulbs next term?" "These sorts of bulbs only grow in the Spring, you will have to wait till next Winter to plant some more." Ruth looks disappointed. The teacher goes on to say, "But I have been thinking we should grow some other kinds of plants in the classroom." "Ooh good!" said Ruth.

<u>March 18th</u>: The class go out for a walk to a nearby hardware shop which also sells seeds, pots and loam, and other garden materials and equipment. They choose some seeds with the advice of the shop assistant who discusses with the teacher the kind of plants which would grow well for the children, germinating quickly and being hardy for planting out during the Easter holidays.

<u>March 20th</u>: The children compare, sort, and examine the seeds with magnifying glasses. They read what they can of the instructions on the seed packets. They are going to take turns to plant some seeds of their choice in containers when they remember to bring these from home.

Comments on Ruth's learning in Example 2

Ruth's experience throughout the Spring term has moved her thinking on from Level 1 to Level 2 in respect of the attainment target on plant growth. The progression she shows is gradual and based on personal experience and a growing interest. She made a book (with drawings and writing) about her daffodil's growth, starting in December with the planting of the bulb and making diary-type entries as the plant grew until late in the Spring term.

It is important to note that if the teacher had given a class lesson in November on plant growth, aimed at the whole of the class, Darren would have quickly become bored and inattentive because he would already have known most of the information. Ruth would also have become bored and inattentive because she would not have been able to relate the knowledge to any personal experience. The story for the other children might have been similar, with only a very few children gaining any new understanding.

It is typical of young children that experience is built up over weeks and months, interest is generated and sustained through the interaction with the teacher, and knowledge is acquired, sometimes in small increments, and at other times through considerable leaps of understanding, <u>as it is relevant to their experience</u>. The teacher's role is responsive to each child's situation. However, this does not mean that children with little relevant experience from outside school (like the example of Ruth and the plants) need to remain behind others with much experience (like Darren). Where children's learning experiences have not prepared them for a particular aspect of school learning, it is important that teachers do not allow their expectations of children to be influenced by social class, ethnic or gender bias. In the case of children with little experience relevant to the particular learning, for whatever reasons, the teacher can usually provide the necessary real experience in school.

Example 2 continued

The story might continue thus: Ruth becomes very keen on plants. By the end of the school year she has developed to a Level 2 understanding of living things, being especially knowledgeable about plants. During the Summer term a few interested children plant out some bedding plants in a small flower-bed in the school grounds. The teacher arranges for the children to make visits to the park as well. These visits are part of a project on the local neighbourhood and the teacher builds on the class's continuing interest in plant life with regular close observation of the flowering and leafing of several different kinds of tree in the park. Some children bring in twigs from trees in their gardens.

The classroom context of example 2

This example of a child's developing understanding can be further appreciated when seen in the context of everyday classroom life and learning. Let us elaborate the case a little further and say that during the school year the children have studied shops, food, plants and the local neighbourhood. They have kept weather charts and thought about the effects of the seasons on their lives, clothing, play outdoors etc. They have looked closely at different vegetables and fruit. These activities were planned mainly in advance by the teacher. In addition, there have been regular weekly cooking sessions with a parent helper. The activities also took place against the background of classroom life described earlier, where children help to clean up after themselves, keep the classroom tidy, and are able to help themselves to many of the resources they need (e.g. paper, pencils, crayons, paint etc.). They have also been making the kinds of choices of activity described when they have used water, blocks, home corner, etc. The events described in this second example would not be unusual in the school year of any nursery or infant class.

These two examples of children learning have focussed on progression as this takes place in the child through experience in school. Using these examples we turn now to the skills of the teacher as a professional observer of children Without some understanding of the role of observation in teaching young children it is difficult to understand how it is possible to ensure progression in what a class of children know and can do.

Knowing children

The informality of the classroom in the early years allows for a wide range of activity to be undertaken. Children can be active or receptive, in conversation or silent, with others or alone, playing or working, for a long or a short time, and putting great or little effort into what they are doing. The range of activity is important and enables the teacher to observe each child under different circumstances. In this way she can learn about children's preferences, social competence, dispositions, language, and strengths and limitations in attainment. Teaching takes place both incidentally and in planned and directed group activities.

For instance, in the example of progression described earlier, Ruth is directly taught in the bulb planting activity (Dec. 14th), she is observed by the teacher in conversation with Darren about watering (Jan. 15th), she is helped with a problem (Feb. 12th), she is given an opportunity to tell the whole class about what she is learning (Feb. 24th), she is <u>given information</u> in an informal conversation at the beginning of the school day (Mar. 15th), she <u>learns</u> on a visit outside the school (Mar. 19th) and she is <u>taught</u> in a small group doing a guided task (March 20th). On all these occasions the teacher has responded to observed levels of interest and current understanding shown by the child.

Participant observation

Much observation of children by the teacher is <u>participant</u>; it is undertaken in interaction and communication with children. Alongside the children the teacher participates in their experiences in the classroom. Much of this observation is in an important sense <u>dynamic</u>. It involves observing children who are changing day by day in significant ways as they learn with the help of other children and adults. Each observation is quickly followed by others in a rich pattern of progressive change. Most of the teacher's observations are not recorded on paper. This is because teachers make thousands of observations which inform their teaching every day. It is also because observations lead to decisions which in turn change what can be observed. Much of what is to be observed is constantly changing.

However, participant observation also enables teachers to monitor, and, where necessary, to influence the more stable and consistent features of children's development. Children have strengths to build on, problems to cope with, and learning difficulties to overcome which require teachers to design and use policies and strategies which are consistent over time. Sometimes such policies have implications for the children's lives beyond the classroom and are therefore negotiated with parents. Decisions are made and evaluated over periods of weeks and months as well as from day to day. Many of the observations relevant to such professional decisions are recorded in a profile of development which assesses children's progress.

Assessment

Continuous assessment of children's attainment, particularly in language and mathematics, is already undertaken by teachers, as well as assessment in other areas of the curriculum. National assessment policies will fit in well here with current practice. However, knowledge of attainment levels alone does not give the teacher the information necessary to plan for young children's future progress: it is also of critical importance to understand children's development in the areas of physical health, perceptual ability, emotional stability, social competence, eagerness to learn, willingness to persevere, and other characteristics relevant to school progress. In addition to subject knowledge and skills. from the very beginning the youngest children in school are having to develop in ways which enable them to become effective learners within the school context.

Observation and assessment

Assessment in the early years is rarely associated with retrospective concerns or judgements. For example, children are not often assessed after teaching with the purpose of seeing how much they have learned following an activity. In the early years, teachers much more frequently use the assessment to plan in advance appropriate provision for children. Through observation they regularly monitor children's current interests, experience, knowledge, and understanding and adopt teaching strategies in the light of these influential factors in learning. In this account of professional practice in the early years, recommendations are offered on assessment and record keeping. These recommendations are based on a view of what teachers need to know in order to make professional judgements in the promotion of children's learning through the curriculum in the early years.

Record keeping

Record keeping should cover several different aspects of developmental progress to take account of the interrelated needs of young children described in section 1. Records of curriculum subject attainment alone are of limited use to teachers planning future learning programmes because they do not provide reasons for the level of attainment of a child nor do they explain problems of attainment. It is essential, however, that record keeping for the "teachers' assessments over time and in normal learning contexts" (TGAT para 16) should not become unrealistically onerous.

The information to be recorded

Each of these four types of record is concerned with different information:

1. Information and insights shared and produced collaboratively between parents and staff, which help to build a more complete picture of the child at home and school.

2. Progress in a child's development as an effective learner in school, through a variety of activities, for example, play, investigation, construction, first hand experience of real world objects and events, negotiation and talk. Progress should be noted in the areas of physical development, health, social competence, motivation, attitudes and dispositions. Clearly comment here would need to be focussed for each child on main strengths and difficulties, those positively or negatively affecting progress. Children's own views of their learning can also be included here.

3. Progress in attainment in the skills and concepts of the curriculum subjects. Progress in the development of ideas about the world and ability to represent and express these in a variety of ways.

4. Class curriculum provision: planning, implementation and evaluation.

All four types of record keeping described here are currently in use in many nursery and infant schools. It would cause considerable concern if records of attainment (type 3) became so detailed that other types of record were no longer kept.

Assessment to enhance effective teaching

Teachers of young children have to be aware of the development of the whole child as a person. All aspects of the young child's functioning are interdependent and any one can facilitate or constrain the development of ability or attainment. As children grow older it is more possible to consider some functioning as of less immediate concern to the teacher. For example, physical or social needs can increasingly be deferred to the demands of classroom study. In the case of the youngest children, however, it is of critical importance for healthy and productive living and learning that teachers do not lose sight of the general picture in pursuit of detailed information exclusively about what children know and can do in the subjects of the curriculum. In the end it is also the quality of the curriculum in the broadest sense which is monitored by means of assessment.

THE LINKS BETWEEN THE PRINCIPLES AND PRACTICE OF EARLY YEARS EDUCATION AND THE INTENTIONS OF THE NATIONAL CURRICULUM

The documents published by the National Curriculum Council are very encouraging in the way in which they explicitly endorse good primary practice. A number of ideas which permeate these documents assert and affirm the very principles on which the early years curriculum is founded.

These ideas include the following:-

1. The starting points are individual children and their environment.

2. Children develop through making meaningful choices and sharing responsibility in relation to their learning.

3. Children learn from first hand experience.

4. There should be a variety of responses to starting points.

5. A cross curricular approach to learning should be encouraged.

6. Children should be given time to produce work of quality and depth.

> (These ideas were developed by Warwickshire County Council Primary Inspectorate and are reported in Campbell and David 1989)

Very positive links can be made between these ideas and the theory, principles and practice for effective education in the early years which have been outlined in this document.

The national curriculum has helped in clarifying the content of the curriculum. It is important for children that early years practitioners continue to developtheir understanding of curriculum processes within an appropriate context for learning.

This paper is a contribution to the debate.

Bibliography

Blenkin, G.M. & Kelly, A.V. (Eds.) (1987). Early Childhood Education: A Developmental Curriculum. London: Paul Chapman

Bruce, T. (1987). Early Childhood Education. London: Hodder and Stoughton

Calderhead, J. (Eds.) (1987). Exploring Teachers' Thinking. London: Cassell

Campbell, R.J. & David, T. University of Warwick (1989). The use of the School and Environment as a Resource for Pupil Learning (unpublished)

Clark, M.M. (1988). Children Under Five: Educational Research and Evidence. London: Gordon and Breach

Cleave, S., Jowett, S., Bate, M. (1979) And So to School - a Study of Continuity from Pre-School to Infant School NFER Nelson

Cohen, D. (1987). The Development of Play. Croom Helm 1987

Curtis, A. (1986). A Curriculum for the Pre-School Child. NFER Nelson

D.E.S. (1988). Report of the Task Group on Assessment and Testing

Donaldson, M. (1978). Children's Minds. Glasgow: Fontana

Dowling, M. (1988). Education 3 to 5: A Teacher's Handbook. Paul Chapman

Hughes, M. (1986). Children and Number. Blackwell Press

Katz, L.G. (1985). Dispositions in Early Childhood Education. ERIC/EECE Bulletin 18 (2), 1.3

Katz, L.B. & Chard S.C. (1989) Engaging the Minds of Young Children: The Project Approach. New Jersey: Ablex

NFER/SCDC (1987). Four Year Olds in School: Policy and Practice

Reynolds, J. & Saunders, M. (1987). Teacher responses to curriculum policy: Beyond the 'delivery' metaphor. In J. Calderhead (Ed.) Exploring Teachers' Thinking. London: Cassell

Tizard, B. & Hughes, M. (1984). Young Children Learning. Glasgow: Fontana

Tizard, B. et al (1988). Young Children at School in the Inner City. Lawrence Erlbaum Associates

Webb, L. (1974). Purpose and Practice in Nursery Education. Blackwell

Wells, G. (1986). The Meaning Makers: Children Learning Language and Using Language to Learn. London: Hodder and Stoughton

Whitehead, M. (1988). Testing... Testing... Can a Broadly Based Early Years Curriculum Survive the Introduction of Testing for Seven Year Olds? Curriculum. Vol. 9, no. 2, 69-73

Wood, D. (1988). How Children Think and Learn. Basil Blackwell